Twayne's United States Authors Series

Sylvia E. Bowman, *Editor*

INDIANA UNIVERSITY

Robinson Jeffers

ROBINSON JEFFERS

By FREDERIC I. CARPENTER

University of California, Berkeley

COLLEGE & UNIVERSITY PRESS · *Publishers*

NEW HAVEN, CONN.

Distributed by

GROSSET & DUNLAP

NEW YORK

I, driven ahead on undiscovered ways
Yet predetermined, do not fail to see,
Over the fog and dust of dream and deed,
The holy spirit, Beauty, beckoning me.

JEFFERS, "Ode on Human Destinies"

Acknowledgments

I gratefully acknowledge the permission of Robinson Jeffers and of Random House, Inc., to quote throughout this book from the volumes of Jeffers' poetry to which they hold copyright. I especially appreciate Mr. Jeffers' kind permission to quote from personal letters.

For their many helpful suggestions concerning the manuscript of this book, I would thank Travis M. Bogard, Robert McNulty, and, last but not least, my wife.

Contents

Introduction

THE FIGURE of Robinson Jeffers is one of the most interesting in contemporary literature. This is a statement of fact, not a value judgment: it does not imply that his poetry is very good or very bad, but rather that it has been called both (embellished with other more emphatic adjectives). In the Conclusion I shall attempt a critical estimate of Jeffers' poetry. This Introduction will keep to the facts, to suggest why the poet is exceptionally interesting.

Few other figures in contemporary literature have endured such extremes of praise and blame in their own lifetimes. For a period of about ten years, from 1925 to 1935, Jeffers was often ranked with T. S. Eliot as our greatest poet and with Eugene O'Neill as our greatest writer of tragedy. But beginning with the Great Depression and continuing through World War II, his critical reputation and popularity alike declined. The author who had been almost universally acclaimed in the 1920's found himself almost universally damned in the 1940's. Such a sudden reversal of literary fortune is rare, and is as interesting as any sudden fall from power. The first chapter of this book will trace and rise and fall of Jeffers' literary reputation as it relates to his own life and to the times he lived in.

Confronted with such a historical phenomenon, the critic seeks reasons for it. What caused this sudden fall from eminence? Were the times at fault? Did the Great Depression and the disastrous world war make the poet's extreme pessimism increasingly unpopular, and his prophecies of doom unendurable? Or was his own later writing at fault: was the decline of his effectiveness (universally admitted) during the war years responsible for discrediting the earlier poetry? Or is all his poetry really as meretricious as his enemies (who had been mostly silent at first) have increasingly asserted? The new critics who came to power in the 1930's chose Jeffers for their whipping boy, and some still consider him "beneath critical notice." These historic questions are central to the study not only of Jeffers but of all modern literature.

Beyond these historic questions, Jeffers' poetry has aroused the greatest critical disagreement, even among his admirers and interpreters. In recent years two books have been published about this poet whom many critics had ceased to mention, and these have praised recent poems which some admirers of his early work dislike. Indeed, those most interested in his poetry have seldom agreed upon the pre-eminence of any one of his poems. Some have praised his earlier adaptations of Greek and biblical myth; others have preferred his narratives of contemporary California; others admire his recent supernatural allegories and fables. Meanwhile some critics and many readers have liked his short poems best and have relegated the more ambitious narratives to the limbo of literary history. The second and third chapters will discuss Jeffers' best poems individually, and seek some common standard for judging them.

It has become increasingly apparent that the sudden changes in Jeffers' reputation, and the sharp disagreements concerning his poetry, have been caused by something more fundamental than changing tastes or critical opinions. The basic problem involves the poet's philosophy of life, or morality, or religion. Many critics have violently denounced Jeffers because he himself has violently denounced the human race. Many moralists have condemned his poetry because of its apparent immorality. Many religious people have been shocked by his attacks not only upon Christianity but upon all great religions of the world. Repeatedly, the charge of "nihilism" has been hurled at his philosophy. And more recently his own adoption of the term Inhumanism has done little to improve the situation. The poet and his critics have increasingly sought to describe this new "ism." The fourth chapter of this book will attempt to clarify the implications of his philosophy.

Meanwhile all critics and readers of his poetry have agreed upon one characteristic of it. The poet himself initially claimed for "Tamar," his first successful poem, the virtue of "singularity." His friend George Sterling early declared that "One could pick out, unerringly, a poem by him from a stock of thousands of others." Since then almost every reader has felt instinctively that all his mature poems bear the stamp of a unique personality, that they seem unmistakably his own. His most recent critic has quoted Henry James (who would almost certainly have disapproved of Jeffers) to describe this virtue: *

* Sidney B. Moss, in *The American Book Collector*, X (September 1959), 9-14. Quoted from Henry James, "The Art of Fiction."

> The only obligation to which in advance we may hold a novel
> . . . is that it be interesting. . . . The ways in which it is
> at liberty to accomplish this result (of interesting us) strike me
> as innumerable. . . . They are as various as the temperament
> of man, and they are successful in proportion as they reveal a
> particular mind, different from others.

Like James's ideal novels, Jeffers' poems are interesting because
they give expression to a "singular," or "particular," mind.
Whether this mind is noble, like that of Milton, or immoral,
like that of the Marquis de Sade, is, for the moment, beside
the question. Jeffers' poetry does successfully "reveal a particular
mind, different from others."

But of course the figure of Jeffers would never have become
so interesting if his mind had described only conventional ideas
in conventional language. What makes his poetry challenging
is that it has always dared to follow his thought to its end,
wherever it might lead. And what has made it disturbing is that
it has often led to dangerous ground, where the slough of
despond may engulf, or the snows of Kilimanjaro may kill. Like
other literary explorers, he has visited the dark continents of the
mind, and his characters have journeyed to the end of the night.

"Beware," warned Emerson over a century ago, "when the
great God lets loose a thinker on this planet." And readers of
Jeffers should beware, for he has followed the directions which
Emerson described but failed to follow. "He who would gather
immortal palms must not be hindered by the name of goodness,
but must explore if it be goodness." Exploring the ultimate ways
of evil, Jeffers' Tamar became the Devil's child, and lived, then,
from the Devil. "You take your way from man," wrote Emerson,
"not to man." And Jeffers has preached "inhumanism." But in
these transcendental regions of the mind, "all things swim and
glitter." Seeking to explore the ultimates of human experience,
Jeffers has seen truth itself to be ambiguous, and he has felt
the deepest emotions of man to be ambivalent. Like Melville's
Taji, he has had "eternity in his eye"; but like Melville's Pierre,
he has often achieved only "a redeeming despair." The singular
mind's journey to the end of the night is always interesting, but
always dangerous. The warnings which the moralistic criticism
of Yvor Winters first aimed at Emerson now apply with even
greater force to Jeffers, for his singularity is the absolute self-
reliance of transcendental individualism in its most extreme form.

Of course the permanent literary value of Jeffers' poetry (as opposed to its historic or psychological interest) must be measured by the standards of objective criticism. But the unique nature of his poetry and the appeal of its controversial individualism also emphasize the importance of the subjective reactions of individual readers to it. From the first, Jeffers' poems have aroused intense reactions in individual readers, and they have merely repelled others. In the course of a lifetime's interest in this poetry, I have heard of many such personal experiences of it, often from casual and non-literary readers. The appeal of the poetry is often immediate, personal, and fundamentally prerational. My own early experience may illustrate.

About 1928, I first read the *Roan Stallion* volume in graduate school, with considerable enthusiasm but with no particular effort to remember it. Many months later I found myself walking across a New England field enjoying an escape from books. Suddenly from under my feet a meadowlark flushed, whirring up with a loud beat of wings. My startled nerves had not quieted when a phrase flashed through my mind: "death's a fierce meadowlark." —No context, no meaning, only the affective experience related unconsciously and immediately to a casual, earlier reading. Only later did I leaf back to rediscover the phrase in the short poem "Wise Men in their Bad Hours," where the metaphor realizes the poet's comparison of the human race to a swarm of grasshoppers—a comparison probably suggested in turn by La Fontaine's fable of the grasshopper and the ant. But the sudden experience of unconscious recall had been literary criticism at its most instinctive—and perhaps at its most effective—before conscious thought or logical analysis had been able to mediate it. And this immediate, personal experience of the value of Jeffers' poetry has often been repeated in different forms by different readers. These actual experiences, more than any abstract studies, have helped to keep Jeffers' poetry alive through recent decades when the negative judgments of conventional critics have threatened to kill it.

Like these unconscious experiences, but more literary, are the borrowings and unconscious quotations of phrases from Jeffers by many modern writers. Often his metaphors have seemed to realize the attitudes of modern man so vividly that they have become part of the language. For example, the phrase "the torches of violence" has made visual one of the most characteristic attitudes of modern history. And Jeffers' title phrase "the tower beyond tragedy" has made concrete the whole underlying idea of his philosophy, as well as of the poem which first suggested it. Metaphors like these have stuck in the mind after the poems that included them have been forgotten: they have been experienced and continue to exist as literary facts.—But the question of why "torches of violence" may be a perfect poetic phrase, and why it transcends technical excellence to imply a larger criticism of life as a whole, is beyond the scope of this Introduction.

Chronology

1887   John Robinson Jeffers, first child of William Hamilton Jeffers and Annie Robinson Tuttle Jeffers, born January 10, in Pittsburgh, Pennsylvania.

1894   Brother, Hamilton Jeffers, born.

1899-
1902   Travel and education in Europe.

1903   Family moved to Pasadena, California. Entered Occidental College.

1905   Graduated Occidental College.

1906   Graduate study at University of Southern California.

1907   Travel in Europe. Studied medicine at U.S.C.

1910   Withdrew from medical school; studied forestry at University of Washington.

1911   Returned to Los Angeles.

1912   Published *Flagons and Apples*. Returned to Washington.

1913   Married Una Call Kuster, August 2, Tacoma, Washington.

1914   Moved to Carmel, California. His father died. His infant daughter, Maev, died.

1916   *Californians* published. Twin sons Donnan and Garth born.

1919   "Tor House" begun.

1921   His mother died.

1924   *Tamar and Other Poems*.

1925   *Roan Stallion, Tamar and Other Poems*.

1927   *The Women at Point Sur*.

1928   *Cawdor and Other Poems*.

1929   *Dear Judas and Other Poems*. Travel with family in Great Britain and Ireland.

1930   Visit to New Mexico.

1931   *Descent to the Dead* published.

1932   *Thurso's Landing and Other Poems.*

1933   *Give Your Heart to the Hawks.*

1935   *Solstice and Other Poems.*

1937   *Such Counsels You Gave to Me.* Travel in Europe.

1938   *The Selected Poetry of Robinson Jeffers* published.

1941   *Be Angry at the Sun.* Trip to eastern cities, and readings of his poetry.

1946   *Medea* published.

1947   *Medea* produced in New York; *Dear Judas* produced.

1948   *The Double Axe and Other Poems.* Travel in Europe.

1950   Una Jeffers died. *Tower Beyond Tragedy* produced in New York.

1954   *Hungerfield and Other Poems* published.

1962   Robinson Jeffers died January 20, in Carmel, California.

Robinson Jeffers

CHAPTER 1

Life and Times
of Robinson Jeffers

R OBINSON JEFFERS, born thirteen years before the twentieth century began, was educated in the era of optimism preceding World War I. This war caused in him an acute psychological crisis which led through a kind of counter-conversion to a sudden literary maturity. After the war, he totally rejected the qualified optimism characteristic of the 1920's. And World War II only increased his pessimism. Obviously, most contemporary authors have lived through these same wars, and many have suffered the loss of faith common to their generation. But the violence of Jeffers' pessimism and the intensity of his disillusion were unique. The sources of this violence may be discovered not only in the history of his times but also in the individual circumstances of his life.

When John Robinson Jeffers was born in 1887, his father, William Hamilton Jeffers, A.B., D.D., LL.D., was forty-nine, and his mother, Annie Robinson Tuttle Jeffers, twenty-seven. To a biographer wise after the event, the difference in age of twenty-two years between father and mother may seem one of the most significant facts of his life. One needs invoke no Freudian Oedipus: the vital statistics of his parentage set him apart from the norm. His poems comment bitterly on "the useless beauty of young brides" married to older men. And psychologically, it is significant that his plots imagine the abnormal relations of father and daughter, and of brother and sister, but never of mother and son—the idealistic young heroes of his narratives feel themselves betrayed by a father, or by a young mother (as in *Such Counsels You Gave to Me*). But all are victims of circumstances dictated by their parentage.

William Hamilton Jeffers, however, was a devoted father and an admirable man. He had been a minister, and in 1887 was professor of Old Testament literature at the Western Theological Seminary of Pittsburgh. He had always identified himself with the Presbyterian Church, and his paternal ancestors, although mostly farmers, had been Calvinists for many generations. The ancestry of the poet was deeply religious, but it was religious in a particular pattern—his ancestors remembered preaching like that of Jonathan Edwards, who had likened sinful man to "a loathsome spider" dangled by an angry God over a pit of fire. Although Robinson Jeffers eventually rejected the dogmas of the Christian church and reluctantly renounced his father's faith, he always honored his ancestors. And unconsciously, perhaps, both the prophetic intensity and the violent imagery of his Calvinist inheritance colored the emotional tone of his poetry.

It is obvious that much of this poetry is autobiographical. Many of these poems remember his father, either directly or indirectly. The early sonnet "To His Father" contrasts the quiet calm of the father's Christian faith and "coronal age," with the poet's own "years nailed up like dripping panther hides / For trophies on a savage temple wall." A later poem, "Promise of Peace," idealizes "the heads of strong old age," who "have dealt with life and been attempered by it." (Jeffers later excluded this from his *Selected Poetry*, perhaps because of the idealization.) But many of the father figures who appear in his narrative poems are described as cold, inflexible, distant. Between the extremes of idealization and of alienation, his father became the symbol of a lost faith and a remembered nobility: admired, regretted, but never warmly shared.

For seven years, Robinson Jeffers remained an only child. During this time his father supervised his education, and at five he was learning Greek. During these years his parents took him on trips to England and the Continent. Of these travels the mature poet would "remember three things: a pocketful of snails loosed on the walls of a kindergarten in Zurich, paintings of Keats and Shelley hanging side by side somewhere in London, and Arthur's Seat, the hill about Edinburgh."[1] Typically, these remembered details were either sensuous or explicitly poetic. During his early years and throughout his young manhood, the poet remained solitary and bookish, forced in upon himself by the lack of companions his own age, and by the very devotedness of the attentions of his parents. And when the family spent the summers at their country estate beside the Ohio River, this solitude continued, leading to a deep love of nature. When his only brother, Hamilton Jeffers, was born, the pattern of solitude had already been set.

Of the poet's mother comparatively little has been recorded. Her ancestry was of New England, where the Robinson and Tuttle families had been prominent; but her parents had died early, and she had been reared by wealthy foster parents in Pittsburgh. Friends remembered her as a woman of "dignity, grace and refinement," and of "great charm, with finely matured mind." She was a talented musician (as was the poet's future wife, Una). In later years it is said that "she had faith in Una as one who could bring her son to great accomplishments."[2] Brought up as a privileged but lonely girl, and early married to a wise but much older husband (whom she was to survive by only seven years), her life was devoted—even more deeply than that of most mothers—to her two sons.

Hamilton Jeffers, seven years younger than Robinson, was never an intimate of his brother. An intellectual also, he grew up to become an astronomer and was later associated with Lick Observatory. The poet shared his brother's enthusiasm for the stars, and later visited him at work: "Our minds have looked / Through . . . the telescope-slotted observatory eyeball, there space and multitude came in / . . . And the earth is a particle of dust by a sand-grain sun . . ." The astronomer's trans-human point of view became the poet's also. But the relationship of the two brothers remained mostly of "our minds."

From the age of seven to fifteen, the poet's education by his father continued (with occasional natural rebellions against paternal authority, and against excessive study). He attended several private schools in Pittsburgh and its suburbs. But when his parents left for extended travels in Europe and in the Near East, he was again uprooted and sent to a succession of boarding schools in Switzerland and Germany for a period lasting three years. During these years Jeffers' life consisted mostly of reading books and of solitary hiking and swimming in the country. With no continuous periods in which to make secure friendships with children his own age and living constantly in alien lands, he was forced in upon himself and books, and outward upon nature. At fifteen, on returning to America, he entered the University of Western Pennsylvania. The bewildering kaleidoscope of experience was revolving fast; but the greatest change was yet to come.

I *West*

In 1903, when he was sixteen years old, the Jeffers family left Pittsburgh and moved to Pasadena, California: Dr. Jeffers' health required the warmer climate. And in California the poet immediately entered Occidental College—a small, quiet, Presbyterian institution, situated near the foot of the mountains—as a third-year student. The same pattern of education which he had followed in the past continued. But the move to this western community, not far from the Pacific Ocean, was to prove momentous. In coming to this far West which he had never seen, he was, strangely, coming "home."

In a purely physical sense, California was to become his permanent home as no other place ever had been before. After living in a series of homes in and about Pittsburgh and attending a series of schools; after traveling about Europe and the Near East; and after being uprooted almost every year, his family now settled down, and he experienced for the first time a sense of permanence. For the rest of his life he was to live in the West, mostly in California. All future travels were to be brief visits to alien places, from which he was to see this new home in perspective.

But in a much deeper and more important sense, California now became the poet's spiritual home. Gradually he came to identify himself with the place, both physically and imaginatively. Indeed, his whole poetry may be read as a symbolic exploration and literary description of the meaning of the far West. And his identification with this West involved a renunciation and symbolic rejection of his earlier life, of the American East, and of Europe. He entitled his second volume of poems *Californians*, and after that he wrote almost constantly of the California coast and its people.

The meanings which California and the West were to assume in his poetry were subtle and manifold. The first and most popular was to be described in the poems: "Continent's End" and "The Torch-Bearers' Race." The latter begins with the flat statement: "Here is the world's end." Then it identifies the poet with the place: "I am building a thick stone pillar upon this shore, the very turn of the world, the long migration's / End." And then it goes on to develop the metaphor of a torch-bearers' race to suggest the westward movement of the world's civilizations, until now the farthest west of these faces at last "the final Pacific." In terms of human history, therefore, the California coast represents "the world's end"; but in terms of cosmic time this human episode pales into insignificance. Addressing the ocean at "Continent's End," the poet imagines her indifference to human history: "The long migrations meet across you and it is nothing to you, you have forgotten us, mother." Settled for his brief lifetime on the far edge of the westernmost continent, gazing across the Pacific toward Asia, the young poet saw himself and his country in the long perspective of history.

But the exact moment of history in which the Jeffers family moved to California was a significant one. In 1903 the state was still sparsely populated: "the West" still preserved a genuine quality of "the wild." The feeling of unsettled newness, experienced suddenly by the young man accustomed to the sophisticated cities of the East and of Europe, was exciting. From the time of his arrival in California he was to identify himself progressively not only with the place but with the time of his first coming to it. "The West" meant wild country, cattle ranches, rugged mountains, and a way of life not yet determined by the routines of civilization nor limited by the pressures of overpopulation. And this ideal moment of the West, when only the forefront of "the last migration" had reached the Pacific, was also in a sense "home." Repeatedly his poems dream the destruction of a later western civilization: "the plaster is all run to the sea and the steel / All rusted; the foreland resumes / The form we loved when we saw it." "The West" meant also the moment of first discovery.

While attending Occidental College, and indeed during all the rest of his life, Jeffers frequently climbed and camped in the western mountains. His love of wild nature, which had begun in the East and grown during his years in Switzerland, now became a dominant characteristic. A classmate remembers him "swinging along over the mountain trails . . . with two or three frying pans that banged and clattered with every step he took, hatless, and bursting every now and then into a long quotation of poetry from Tennyson or Homer." And as time went on, these mountains became almost an obsession with him. In his early volume, *Californians*, a poem begins: "He has fallen in love with the mountains: / How should he not be blest?" And through his later poetry the wild setting of the narratives often dwarfs the human action. Finally, at the end of *The Double Axe*, a visionary horseman imagines that he sees three hills "like Red Indians around a campfire" sitting as "Inquisitors" and examining the remains of the last men destroyed by the bomb.

Interpreted in terms of literary history, this love of mountains and wild nature may be simply romantic; and there is much of Wordsworth and Byron in the poetic temperament of Jeffers. Some of his best short poems are idylls of nature, describing "All the Little Hoof-Prints." Some of his most powerful poems repeat "the pathetic fallacy" and impute human emotions to nature: "The sad red splendid light beats upward / These granite gorges . . ." Both his personal temperament and his poetry explicitly scorn "humanity" with a Byronic intensity. And both his actual life and his philosophy were to repeat Emerson's rejection of society: "Good-bye, proud world, I'm going home." But the mountains and the wild nature, which Jeffers had first learned to love in the East and in Europe, were to take on new meanings in the West; these were to go beyond literary Romanticism to approach a philosophic naturalism.

About the same time Jeffers was exploring his California country, another easterner with a European background was proclaiming the philosophy of naturalism to a University of California audience. In 1911 George Santayana suggested how Californians, in particular, might transcend "The Genteel Tradition in American Philosophy":[3]

> When you escape, as you often do, to your forests and your Sierras, I am sure that you do not feel you made them, or they were made for you. . . . In their non-human beauty and peace they stir the sub-human depths and the super-human possibilities of your own spirit. . . . It is the yoke of this genteel tradition itself that these primeval solitudes lift from your shoulders.

Whether or not Jeffers read Santayana's words, they prophesied with astonishing accuracy the development of his life and his poetic thought. For him the wild nature of the California mountains not only stirred "the sub-human depths and the super-human possibilities" of the spirit but broke the bonds of "the European genteel tradition" in which he had been brought up.

The liberal philosophy of naturalism, which Santayana prophesied, was to fascinate Jeffers, and we shall consider it in a later chapter. But the actual liberating influence of the western land upon the eastern mentality was having its immediate effect upon Jeffers' life. Santayana had traced the American source of genteel tradition to the "agonized conscience" of the New England Puritans: Jeffers' father had been a Calvinist minister, and his mother had been brought up in the more social amenities of the genteel tradition. Now the family's move to the West coincided with the son's adolescent revolt from paternal authority to produce a total revolt from tradition. While attending Occidental College, he ceased to live at home. And after his graduation, when his parents had taken him with them on another trip to Europe, he suddenly decided to return to California alone. And for eight years he continued to live in the West: homeless, unsettled, disturbed, lonely, but with "the wild wine freedom on his lips." The West, which meant first "the long migration's end," and then the moment of first discovery, and again the wildness of unsettled nature, now suggested the spirit of freedom itself.

All these aspects of western life influenced Jeffers and informed his later poetry. But beyond these was the very quality of the poetic imagination which this life in the new West stirred. After the kaleidoscopic changes of his youth and the sudden move to the West, his imagination now projected itself upon the future. Using the concrete materials of the actual West—the granite mountains, the ocean beaches, the burning sun, and the coastal fog—the young poet dreamed himself beyond these. And the "Epilogue" to his first, youthful volume of poems consciously described this final "West":

> For our country here at the west of things
> Is pregnant of dreams; and west of the west
> I have lived; where the last low land outflings
> Its yellow-white sand to the edge of the bay;
> And the west wind over us every day
> Blows, and throws with the landward spray
> Dreams on our minds, and a dreamy unrest.
>
> The westward sea and the warm west wind—
> It was these, not I, that wrought my rhyme.
> I, that have lived, and sorrowed, and sinned,
> Have spoken no word of my life as it is;

Have spoken only the ocean's abyss,
Only the open waves, that kiss,
And climb on the cliff, and fall, and climb.

But in following the poetic meanings of the "wild" West in which Jeffers now lived, we have omitted the more prosaic details. During his two years at Occidental College he distinguished himself as a student, he was well liked by his classmates, and he contributed to and edited the college magazines. His poems in *The Aurora* and *The Occidental*, written between the ages of sixteen and eighteen, are excellent if judged by undergraduate standards. In 1904 a poem entitled "The Condor" was published by *The Youth's Companion.*⁴ Indeed, from his earliest college years he devoted himself wholeheartedly and single-mindedly to the vocation of poetry, and from the beginning he achieved success in it.

But the life of a poet has seldom been easy, and for eight years Jeffers was to live uneasily. If his existence was made simpler by the financial support of his parents and relatives, it was made more difficult by his continuing revolt from parental standards. During the eight years between his graduation from college, at the age of eighteen, and his marriage, he tried many ways of life, explored many new places and new ideas, and struggled constantly to find his true self: "I, Father, having followed other guides / And oftener to my hurt no leader at all . . ." These long years of being lost and of searching blindly for some unknown goal were to leave their indelible imprint on his poetry.

But the central problem—and in a sense the only problem—of these years was caused by his love for his future wife. After entering the University of Southern California graduate school in 1905, he soon met a fellow student of literature, Una Call Kuster. An attractive and widely admired young woman and two years his senior, she was married to a lawyer, Edward Kuster. Una Kuster loved poetry, was attracted by the brilliance of the young poet, and lent him a book about Wordsworth. He, shy and unsure of himself, admired her social maturity and self-assurance, and fell in love. The relatives and friends of each tried to break up what seemed an infatuation. The distress and disapproval of Dr. and Mrs. Jeffers were extreme. When the young people's love continued, and Una spoke of divorce, she was sent to visit relatives in the East, and later to spend a year in Europe; Jeffers first went to Europe with his parents, then suddenly returned, and later moved to the University of Washington in Seattle. Both struggled without success against their deep attraction. To us, half a century later, living in a society in which the relativity of moral standards has become more widely recognized, their problem remains clear; but in the early years of the century the son of a Christian minister seemed bent on denying the very foundations of his society. It is hard to overestimate the intensity of the period of *Sturm und Drang* through which the young poet lived.

During these eight years Jeffers studied various subjects in various graduate schools, but must important to his future poetry was his study of medicine. After attending the University of Zurich briefly, he returned from Europe and re-enrolled in the University of Southern California; this time not in letters, but in the college of medicine. Never intending tc become a doctor, he was interested primarily in science and in the scientific point of view. But he disciplined himself to memorize all the details of anatomy as well as the larger principles of science; and his later poetry is full of the vocabulary of physiology, as well as the ideas of the scientist. The chief character of "Margrave," a later poem, is a medical student:

> He saw clearly in his mind the little
> Adrenal glands perched on the red-brown kidneys, as
>   if all his doomed tissues became transparent,
> Pouring in these passions their violent secretion
> Into his blood-stream, raising the tension unbearably.
>   And the thyroids; tension, tension.

Sometimes this scientific language seems intrusive—just as his medical study seems an interlude in a life devoted to literature —but sometimes it makes vivid the emotion and enlarges the horizon. And in actual life the study of medicine served to draw him out of the aestheticism which characterized so many of the poets of his time and to focus his interest on the modern world. While in medical school he lived in the home of his professor of bacteriology, was engaged in competitive athletics, and won the heavyweight wrestling championship of the university. If he tended to withdraw increasingly into himself, socially, he kept actively in contact with the world about him.

II *Flagons and Apples*

Meanwhile his emotional conflict drove him to the irregular life and occasional excesses characteristic of many youthful and romantic poets. During summer vacations he roomed in a cottage at Hermosa Beach and hobnobbed with fishermen and long-shoremen. In a later account of his "First Book" he describes how he lost an early manuscript of *Flagons and Apples* while drinking until the early hours at a saloon. And his later sonnet-series on "The Truce and the Peace" recreates the physical turmoil and psychological confusion of these years, although he projected it in imagination at the end of World War I—when he had, in actuality, long since ended his *wanderjahre* with an ideally happy marriage.

In 1912 a small legacy from his grandfather allowed Jeffers to finance the publication of his first volume of poetry by a small Los Angeles company. In this small volume the poems are for the most part conventional, late-Victorian lyrics, with titles such as "To Aileen-of-the-Woods." They reflect the poetic en-thusiasms of his youth, which included Dante Gabriel Rossetti, Swinburne, and George Moore. Except for the "Epilogue" (which we have already quoted), neither the style nor the substance of these poems gives any premonition of the originality and power which were to come, and there is no reason to doubt his own account of them: "Something was said at the printing-shop about sending out review copies; but my interest in the book was waning, the irrational need for publication seemed to be satisfied by the printing, and nothing further was done."

Perhaps the most interesting passages in the volume are its introductory mottoes: from the *Song of Songs*, "Stay me with flagons, comfort me with apples: for I am sick of love"; and from R. W. Emerson, "And ever the Daemonic Love / Is the ancestor of wars, / And the parent of remorse." *Flagons and Apples* marked the end of his youth, when he had become sick of light loves; the violent psychological struggle to attain his true love had stirred the depths of his being.

After three years of studying medicine in Los Angeles, Jeffers entered the school of forestry at the University of Washington; after a year there, he returned to Los Angeles; then he went again to Seattle. But finally, in 1913, Una Kuster obtained her divorce; and on August 2, she and Jeffers were married. Eight years of struggle and uncertainty had preceded a marriage which was to prove as perfect as any in the history of literature.

In every way Una Jeffers was a remarkable woman, as all who knew her have borne witness. And her relation to her husband became profound and many-sided. " 'She gave me eyes, she gave me ears, and she arranged my life,' " he wrote, quoting Wordsworth's testimony to his sister. A lifelong lover of poetry, Una became at once inspiration and audience, secretary and critic. Her social energy constantly drew him out of his natural introversion and brought him into contacts with people; yet, when he attained fame, she also protected him from interruption and distraction. Every correspondent of his has received as many letters from her in his name as from him. More important, she gave him the assurance he needed: besides wife, she became both sister and mother, confidante and friend. But most important of all, she entered into his imagination to become a personal presence in his poems: without ostentation or sentimentality his wife shares in the narrative and lyric projections of his mind, as in "An Artist" and "A Redeemer." In literature as in life, she gave reality to what might have remained, without her, shadowy figments of the imagination.

It is perhaps natural that so remarkable a woman should have become the subject of a book: *Of Una Jeffers*, by Edith Greenan. The significant facts include her Irish ancestry and temperament, which was spontaneously and frankly emotional, and her love of folk poetry and music. Her father had been a sheriff in Michigan, and she had come to Los Angeles as a child. During her first marriage, as always, she had been loved and admired. After her marriage to Jeffers, the two lived briefly in his mother's house, for no ill will remained from the years of parental opposition to their marriage. And after their settlement in Carmel, friends and visitors came to see her as well as him.

But the most remarkable fact about the brief biography of Una Jeffers is its authorship: Edith Greenan was the second wife of Edward Kuster. And these two women became lifelong friends. As Jeffers wrote in a foreword to the volume: "thirty years ago, this friendship would have been impossible." Much more interesting than any facts of Una Jeffers' life is the utter sincerity of this tangled relationship, and the light it throws, indirectly, on the poet's own problems. When Edith Greenan met Una Kuster and Robinson Jeffers at the urging of Edward

Kuster, emotional and social problems were acute. When, many years later, she visited them in Carmel, each had found his own happiness, and society had accepted their new order.

> Praise youth's hot blood if you will, I think
> that happiness
> Rather consists in having lived clear through
> Youth and hot blood, on to the wintrier hemisphere
> Where one has time to wait and to remember.

The year following their marriage was one of indecision: they considered living in Europe, but returned for a time to Los Angeles, where their first child, Maev, was born. But the infant lived only a few days, and about then war broke out in Europe. "The August news turned us to this village of Carmel instead; and when the stage-coach topped the hill from Monterey, and we looked down through pines and sea-fogs on Carmel Bay, it was evident that we had come without knowing it to our inevitable place." They rented a cottage in the pines and lived there for several years. Later Jeffers bought several acres of land overlooking the ocean at the edge of the village and began building "Tor House," where he has lived ever since. Symbolically, after twenty-seven years of wandering, the poet built his permanent home of sea-worn granite facing "the final Pacific." Then gradually as poem after poem celebrated the wild beauty of Carmel and of the mountains to the south, this became "Jeffers country" as completely and inevitably as Egdon Heath had become "Hardy country" before.

But this Carmel country, which became home both to the poet and his characters, is much more than a geographical place— although Jeffers himself specifically so described it in a prose "Note About Places" appended to his *Californians* and although his biographer, Powell, located on his map in detail the different events of the narrative poems. The country is overwhelmingly beautiful, but it is far more than a mere setting of natural beauty: "Here the human past is dim and feeble and alien to us / Our ghosts draw from the crowded future," the poet wrote in "Haunted Country." And yet the human past is more real on the Monterey peninsula than in any other place in the West. And the associations of human history, although mostly "alien to us," have made Carmel the literary capital of the West.

Addressing "A Rock that Will Be a Cornerstone of the House," Jeffers asked: "How long a time since the brown people who have vanished from here / Built fires beside you and nestled by you / Out of the ranging sea-wind?" And in one of the strangest incidents in that strange poem, *Tamar*, his heroine descends at night to the sea beach to perform an obscene dance, in which she imagines herself violated by the spirits of the Indians who had lived here before the white man destroyed them.

After the Indians, of course, the Spaniards came to Christianize this place, and founded their capital in Monterey. Richard Henry Dana, who sailed up the coast described the scene in *Two Years Before the Mast*, which Jeffers read. But the bitter ironies of the Spanish treatment of the Indians in these lovely "Pastures of Heaven" interested Jeffers less than they did John Steinbeck: the half-breed Spanish characters of Jeffers' poems are mostly contemporary vagabonds who dream confusedly of finding love and salvation in the Carmel wilderness. And the modern California ranchers who people Jeffers' narratives live out their primitive lives against the backdrop of this alien history, which, seemingly forgotten, nevertheless haunts them.

III *Californians*

Happily married and settled in his "inevitable place," Jeffers now devoted himself entirely to the writing of poetry. In 1916 he sent off the manuscript of *Californians* to Macmillan Company in New York; incredibly, it was accepted promptly. The book was published in an attractive format, received few reviews, and was soon forgotten. However, Oscar W. Firkins, discussing it in *The Nation*, had wise and good things to say about it. Firkins compared Jeffers' attitude to Emerson's, observing that each "had a shoulder in his voice" which interfered with the smooth flow of his poetry. But he admired many of Jeffers' poems and predicted a brilliant future for the young poet. Nevertheless, his review remained an isolated oasis for eight years. *Californians* was allowed to go out of print, and until 1925 no major publisher would risk publishing the poet.

It must be admitted that *Californians* got much the treatment it deserved. The poems are uniformly good, but never great. Moreover, they remain largely conventional, offering only

glimpses of a future originality and power. On one hand, they
consist of narratives with California settings, and they sometimes
deal tentatively with the situations of the later, longer narrative
poems. And on the other, they consist of odes and meditative
lyrics which offer fresh but never radical observations and
speculations about the modern world. The narratives, set in
various places which Jeffers had explored in the earlier years of
his wandering, have not yet focused on the "haunted country"
about Carmel. And the speculative poems also reflect the more
romantic—and often vaguely optimistic—ideas typical of American
literature before World War I.

The most ambitious, and in some ways the most interesting
of these early poems, is entitled "Ode on Human Destinies."
Both in style and in content it expresses the ideas characteristic
of Jeffers' early manhood and of the early years of twentieth-
century America. In style, it sometimes imitates the Miltonic,
but sometimes it became original and eloquent. In content, it
sometimes imagines high future events:

> And Man, with unreturning course
> Into the breathless aether force
> His guarded way, and colonize
> A later planet . . .

But it also expresses the sober self-questioning of the young
American facing the threat of new wars recently broken out
across "Europe's blood-wonted boundaries." The poet assures
himself that such wars have occurred before. But then he pro-
claims a faith beyond history:

> Behold, our faith may be even as the Earth's
> Unhopeful and firm-rooted. —The man dies?
> The race is hardly yeaning yet. The race
> At length will perish also? Other births
> Even now are quickening in the timeless womb.
> Life tortures the old clay to later form;
>
> .   .   .   .
>
> Something endures; the universal Power
> Endures forever; we, the whiffs and flames
> That breathe and flicker for one briefest hour,
> We also have our dignity, being part
> Of the immortal thing; . . .

And he ends with the true poet's peroration:

> I, driven ahead on undiscovered ways
> Yet predetermined, do not fail to see,
> Over the fog and dust of dream and deed,
> The holy spirit, Beauty, beckoning me.

This "Ode on Human Destinies" is important because it marks the end of an era, of Jeffers' period of poetic apprenticeship, of a period of American optimism. In it the poet has proclaimed his belief in the infinite potentialities of man, in man's power of endurance despite recurrent wars, and—most of all—in the mission of the poet to worship "Beauty." But during the next eight years Jeffers was to develop a new style of poetry utterly his own. He was to reject not only the youthful optimism of "Human Destinies" but even the older faith in the dignity of man. And finally, his very concept of "the holy spirit, Beauty," was to suffer sea-change in the stormy years ahead.

IV *Awakening*

In 1916 the great war which the young poet had been observing from afar suddenly engulfed America, and Jeffers was faced with the problem of his own relation to it. This was complicated by the birth of twin sons, Garth and Donnan, in November, 1916. Torn between his duty to his wife and children and his duty to enlist, he went through a long period of indecision. In Una Jeffers' words:

> . . . After suffering considerable disturbance of mind, he made various unsuccessful applications for training for a commission; he was examined for aviation and rejected for high blood pressure. However, he had been provisionally accepted for baloon service and was awaiting instructions when peace was declared.

The conflict of motives on the subject of going to war or not was probably one of several factors that, about this time, made the world and his own mind much more real and intense to him. Another factor was the building of Tor House. As he helped the masons shift and place the wind and wave-worn granite I think he realized some kinship with it, and became aware of strengths in himself unknown before. Thus at the age of thirty-one there came to him a kind of awakening such as adolescents and religious converts are said to experience.

This "kind of awakening," or conversion, was beyond question the determining experience of Jeffers' life. But actually this awakening involved two experiences: the first was a long period of indecision and a questioning of the idealisms of the past; the second was a dedication to the actual earth and boulders of the new home which he was laboring to build with his own hands. The first of these experiences was an ambivalent one, which led through confusion and disillusion to a practice of personal isolation and to an eventual preaching of national isolation. The second experience was a positive one; it led away from the romantic aestheticism of his youth toward the practice of manual labor and to the celebration of the active life of the ranchers and sheepherders of his Carmel coast.

Whatever the psychological and moral results of this period of "awakening," the poetic results were both significant and valuable. During these years Jeffers followed the same path of poetic development traced by Whitman the century before. From a minor writer of conventional rhymes and stanzas, Jeffers became an individual poet with mastery over a new medium. But the change was not so sudden as it had seemed in the case of Whitman, and some of the transitional poems have survived.

In 1918 Jeffers wrote "An Alpine Christ," "a long lyrical drama somewhat modeled after Shelley's 'Prometheus,'" and the first of his many narrative poems dealing with the Christ theme. Although he discarded this poem soon after its composition, some of its manuscript pages have been preserved on the back of the work sheets of later poems. The idea of "An Alpine Christ" was to evolve into "The Coast-Range Christ"—a long poem in rhymed couplets included in the later *Tamar* volume. This later volume also included the long sonnet sequence on "The Truce and the Peace," which was also written in these transitional years. Unlike Whitman, whose early poems in conventional forms were uniformly bad, Jeffers wrote much good poetry before abandoning conventional rhyme and metre altogether.

During the eight long years between the publication (and comparative failure) of *Californians* and that of *Tamar*—a period in which Jeffers struggled to develop his own poetic medium and to define his own relation to the world about him, without help or encouragement from anyone except his wife—he found physical occupation, and even a kind of symbolic direction, in working on Tor House. After the end of the war he had contracted for a new house on the new land beside the ocean. But since the contractor was slow, the poet hired himself out as a stone mason, both to help with his own hands and to supervise the general work. Then, after the house itself was finished, he continued for several years to work on the rock tower beside it. Many stories have accumulated concerning this long labor: one tells of a neighbor who went abroad for three years and returned to find Jeffers working in exactly the same position in which he had last seen him three years before. But once the actual house had been completed, the tower—and the physical work upon it—became more symbolic than practical.

The heavy rock tower, "Tor House," embodied many of its maker's ideas, and it has become a kind of literary landmark in the West. It includes a winding stone stairway leading up to the poet's study. In its masonry walls are embedded trophies and keepsakes collected from many lands. From its square ramparts the view stretches south beyond Point Lobos and west to the Pacific horizon. In its solitude and its beauty, it became the physical prototype for the poetic conception of the "Tower Beyond Tragedy." But most of all it became a kind of anchor, or center, for the poet's hitherto scattered and uncentered life. A typical later poem begins by defining this center:

> On the small marble platform
> On the turret on the head of the tower,
> Watching the night deepen.
> I feel the rock-edge of the continent
> Reel eastward with me below the broad stars.
> I lean on the broad worn stones and my hands that
>   touch them reel eastward.
> The inland mountains go down and new lights
> Glow over the sinking east rim of the earth.
> The dark ocean comes up,
> And reddens the western stars with its fog-breath
> And hides them with its mounded darkness.

V *New Forms: Tamar*

While working physically to build "Tor House," Jeffers was also working on his poetry, experimenting with new forms. Several times he collected groups of poems to send off to eastern publishers, but always without success. Seven manuscript title-pages of these projected volumes have survived, and their tables of contents include some of the best poems to be published later—and to receive enthusiastic acclaim—in the *Tamar* volume. The traditional fallibility of commercial publishers finds one more illustration in the paradox that Jeffers' earlier, minor *Californians* had been accepted at once, whereas these new, major poems were uniformly rejected.

In June, 1922, Jeffers collected the best of his poems before "Tamar" in a manuscript volume entitled *Brides of the South Wind*. For it he wrote an important prose Introduction, in which he described clearly his poetic credo. In much the same terms which he was to use in later statements of his poetic theory, he declared his belief in traditional poetry, modified only slightly by temporal fashion and individual practice. We shall consider this poetic theory in a later chapter; but here one statement is important because it defines his ideas and practice at the moment of transition:

> The greatest dramatic poetry in English is not rhymed, the greatest narrative poetry is not rhymed. It may seem strange, in view of my belief, that the narrative poems in this book of mine are rhymed: it is because until quite lately I was unable to discover any rhymeless measure but blank verse that could tell a story flexibly, without excess of monotony. Blank verse I could not use, because it has been so much used by such masters; it carries their impress and inflections. I think I am at length discovering rhymeless narrative measures of my own; but the poems are not finished, and not included in this series.

About 1922 he began writing "Tamar." But after its completion he decided not to offer it to the commercial publishers who had rejected so many earlier collections of his poems. Probably his consciousness that the theme of the title poem might also contribute to its rejection influenced his decision. But as he wrote later, "it seemed to me that the verses were not merely negligible, like the old ones, but had some singularity." And so he decided to publish the volume privately. He sent it to Peter G. Boyle, a New York printer; and, on April 30, 1924, *Tamar and Other Poems* appeared.

The history of this volume in significant, and its vicissitudes suggest the unique nature both of Jeffers' poetry and of his literary reputation. Because Peter Boyle, whom Jeffers had hired as printer, experienced a genuine enthusiasm for the poems, he sent out entirely on his own responsibility many review copies to newspapers and magazines. But none would notice this privately published book; and, after a time, Boyle shipped the remaining 450 copies in "a packing box as big as a coffin" across the continent to the author. Meanwhile Jeffers had been invited to contribute verses to a new anthology of California writers which was to be entitled *Continent's End*. And with the poems which he submitted, he also sent gift copies of his new volume to George Sterling and James Rorty, the editors. They in turn became enthusiastic, and Rorty, a professional journalist traveling to New York, persuaded Mark Van Doren and Babbette Deutsch to read the new volume. The enthusiasm spread, and soon reviews by Rorty, Van Doren, and Deutsch appeared prominently in *The New York Herald Tribune, The Nation,* and *The New Republic.* Peter Boyle suddenly needed copies of *Tamar* to meet the new demand, the packing case was shipped back to New York, and soon the first edition was exhausted.

Tamar and Other Poems, like most of Jeffers' subsequent poetry, possessed the power of exciting tremendous enthusiasm among fellow poets and critics, at the same time that it raised doubts and occasionally violent objections in other—and, indeed, sometimes in the same—individuals. Mark Van Doren's words of acclaim were typical: "Few volumes are as rich with the beauty and strength that belong to genius alone. With Mr. Jeffers, as with other major poets, humanity breaks into fire." The immediate conviction that this poetry was "In Major Mold" found expression by many influential critics, and was repeated by lesser reviewers throughout the nation. In California newspapers and magazines, where local pride magnified the enthusiasm, George Sterling and others praised the volume with superlatives. But at the same time the forbidden themes and the amoral treatment sometimes provoked opposite reactions. A San Francisco parochial paper headlined: "Pagan Horror from Carmel-by-the-Sea"; and it continued: "Robinson Jeffers has the power of Aeschylus, the subtlety of Sophocles. Shelley and Swinburne played at being pagans. This man's work is ruggedly pagan. It is no tour de force. He is intrinsically terrible." Other influential critics such as Floyd Dell adopted a milder form of attack, headlining: "Shell-Shock and the Poetry of Robinson Jeffers." Nevertheless, in the moment of first discovery, the chorus of praise was overwhelming.

After the first, small edition of *Tamar* had been exhausted, the enthusiasm of critics and reading public practically forced an established publisher to take over. But since *Tamar* had been only a slim volume and Jeffers had written many new poems, it was decided to issue a new, combined volume with the title of *Roan Stallion, Tamar, and Other Poems*. This duly appeared under the aegis of Boni and Liveright in November, 1925. The dust wrapper printed new testimonials by Edwin Arlington Robinson and Havelock Ellis, as well as excerpts from reviews by Sterling and Van Doren. After the first printing the phrase of Robinson, "You have an amazing fertility and daring," was omitted because it had been quoted from a personal letter; the parallel with Whitman's famous printing of a personal letter from Emerson is interesting. But in the case of Jeffers a later letter from Robinson reaffirmed the praise.

The *Roan Stallion* volume rapidly achieved a critical and popular success of a degree rare in the annals of poetry; during the following years many editions of the book were printed. With the success of *Roan Stallion*, Jeffers suddenly achieved both recognition and financial reward, although these did not very much affect his solitary life. More anthologies like *Continent's End* and more magazines and newspapers requested poetic contributions from him. A group of his poems—some of them ranking with his best—was published for the first time in *A Miscellany of American Poetry: 1927*. Articles about him began appearing frequently in the national journals. The local *Carmelite* devoted an issue to him. Neighbors such as George Sterling, and Lincoln and Ella Steffens became his admiring friends. Early in 1927 Sterling's enthusiastic vignette of him was published as a book. In August, Charles Cestre published an article, "Robinson Jeffers," in *Revue Anglo-Américaine*. By virtue of a single volume of poetry, and within the brief period of two years, he had achieved international fame. It is interesting to speculate what his reputation might now be had his career ended at this stage.

VI *Critical Doubts: The Women at Point Sur*

In July, 1927, the publication of *The Women at Point Sur* caused many critics to re-examine their earlier praise, and others to emphasize their disapproval. This most violent and unrelieved of all the long poems was received with shock by many and with approval by few. Mark Van Doren commented: "He seems to be knocking his head to pieces against the night." H. L. Davis reaffirmed: "The most splendid poetry of my time"; but he concluded, "and yet—the poem itself is dead." Newspaper reviewers headlined: "Dull Naughtiness," and "Hysterics," and "Happily Not Many Will Read *The Women at Point Sur*." In the *New York Times* Percy Hutchinson explained, "Robinson Jeffers Attempts a New Beauty." But the attempt seemed unsuccessful. In November, 1927, when Benjamin de Casseres published in *The Bookman* the most enthusiastic article on Jeffers yet written, John Farrar replied in later pages of the same magazine: "Jeffers is a good poet. . . . But his growingly idiotic following . . . will praise him into obscurity if they aren't careful."

Cawdor and *Dear Judas*, published in 1928 and 1929, contributed substantially to Jeffers' reputation; they also made clearer the particular nature of that reputation. The fact that *Cawdor* told its story in more realistic detail than the earlier narratives, and with fewer mythical exaggerations, served only to emphasize the story's difference from more normal fictions. And the rejection by *Dear Judas* of the orthodox interpretation of the gospel story inevitably offended many readers. Yet most reviewers welcomed the sympathetic treatment of the theme of self-sacrifice in the twin narratives of "Dear Judas" and "The Loving Shepherdess." And the publication of such shorter poems as "Apology for Bad Dreams" and "A Redeemer," suggested a rationale for the violence of these narratives. A method was becoming apparent in the poetic madness.

In 1929, following the publication of four volumes of poetry in four successive years, Jeffers took a long vacation; and, for the first time in more than twenty years, he traveled abroad. With his wife and sons he visited Great Britain, and then rented a cottage in Ireland, where the family settled for nearly a year. The site had been chosen as the home of Una Jeffers' ancestors, and the poet adopted it, symbolically, as the ancestral home of the race. From this old world, he now looked westward at his own country, and the perspectives became sharper. Having chosen the Far West as his true home, both in fact and in imagination, this return to Great Britain and Ireland became symbolically a "Descent to the Dead." In 1931 the group of poems describing this "descent" was published. And this return to past time, both actual and poetic, marks the mid-point of his career.

The violent denunciation of western civilization, which has characterized all his mature poetry, and the violent tragedies, which his narratives have always imagined for his California coast, tend to obscure not only the genuine love which the poet felt for his land but also the poetic idealization with which he remembered his youthful life upon it. "West of the West" he had lived in the land of freedom, natural beauty, and infinite potentiality. And now from the old world he remembered longingly this early West:

> When you and I on the Palos Verdes cliff
> Found life more desperate than dear,
> And when we hawked it on the lake by Seattle,
> In the West of the world, where hardly
> Anything has died yet . . . .

By contrast he now looked down on this old "Subjected Earth."

> Here all's down hill and passively goes to the grave
> Asks only a pinch of pleasure between the darknesses,
> Contented to think that everything has been done
> That's in the scope of the race. . . .

And from the perspective of this alien old world the poet welcomed the challenge of the new:

> so should I also perhaps
> Dream, under the empty angel of this twilight,
> But the great memory of that unhumanized world,
> With all its wave of good and evil to climb yet,
> Its exorbitant power to match, its heartless passion
> to equal
> And all its music to make, beats on the grave-mound.

If the year 1929 marks the mid-point of Jeffers' career, it also marks a mid-point in American history. And the connection between the two is perhaps closer than it seems. As Radcliffe Squires has pointed out: "If Jeffers' poetry in the 1920's castigated a society whose feelings of guilt demanded the castigation, the whip seemed excessive when an economic depression descended." Jeffers' early narratives not only castigated the naïvely affluent society of the 1920's—they did so with calculated purpose. His prophetic denunciations were inspired by the bloated optimism of the period and were intended to purge it. The bitterness of his medicine only made it seem the more palatable.

Moreover, his shorter poems of this period made explicit his purpose. "Apology for Bad Dreams" explained: "I imagined victims for those wolves, I made them phantoms to follow, / They have hunted the phantoms and missed the house." And he added: "Remembered deaths be our redeemers, / Imagined victims our salvation." More concretely still, a later poem imagined "A Redeemer" who explained:

> . . . I am here on the mountain making
> Antitoxin for all the happy towns and farms, the lovely
>   blameless children, the terrible
> Arrogant cities.

In the 1920's, therefore, Jeffers wrote his prophetic denunciations with a practical purpose—a purpose partly personal, partly social. Like the prophets of the Old Testament, he warned his generation to consider its sins and prepare for its fate. And like these prophets of ancient Israel, he denounced his country because he loved it. Like them he probably realized that his denunciations would be more effective psychologically than practically. But with whatever reservations, his poetry of this period was motivated by some of the idealism which he had earlier attributed to "Woodrow Wilson"—"the great delusion of a major purpose."

On his return to America in 1930, he found his reputation approaching its high point. Besides enthusiastic reviews and general articles, Lloyd Morris' analysis of "The Tragedy of a Modern Mystic" had interpreted Jeffers' poetry with insight and related it to fundamental philosophic problems. In 1931 Benjamin Lehman described it as a new expression of the "neutral" philosophy of modern science, emphasizing "the destruction that inheres in the anthropocentric view." In 1932 Lawrence Clark Powell published the first complete book on Jeffers and his poetry (which remains perhaps the best). And the next year S. S. Alberts published an inclusive *Bibliography of the Works of Robinson Jeffers*. That a full-length bibliography of a contemporary poet should have been issued by a commercial publisher only eight years after the appearance of his first major book of poems is a fact perhaps unique in the history of literature.

Meanwhile Jeffers spent the first of several summer vacations in Taos, New Mexico, in 1930, visiting Mabel Dodge Luhan and other friends of D. H. Lawrence. In 1931 his European poems were published in a limited edition. In 1932 and 1933 *Thurso's Landing and Other Poems,* and *Give Your Heart to the Hawks* were published and were well reviewed. The heroine of the latter narrative embodied most clearly, perhaps, the asocial philosophy of individual freedom and extreme self-reliance which had always been prominent in the author's poetry. The title phrase "Give Your Heart to the Hawks" seemed to sum it all up perfectly.

In 1935 Jeffers' reputation had reached its highest point. Niven Busch, discussing the phenomenon in the *Saturday Review of Literature,* pointed out that "merely in terms of dollars and cents" the manuscripts and first editions of Jeffers were commanding a price higher than those of any contemporary American author. From the first printing of *Roan Stallion,* his poems before their regular publication had regularly been issued in expensive, limited editions signed by the author. His manuscripts were being purchased by major collectors for their libraries. The first editions of his earliest poems were selling for more than similar first editions of many major authors of the nineteenth century. A Jeffers cult, comparable to the Whitman cult which had surrounded the good gray poet during his latter years, was already becoming established. An elderly admirer of Whitman's poetry compared a visit to "Tor House" with his own pilgrimage to Camden of long ago. The aura of immortality seemed already to have invested the modern poet.

VII   *Decline of a Reputation*

But in 1935 Jeffers' reputation had already begun to decline. The great depression certainly contributed to this unpopularity, for violent tragedy seems acceptable only in times of comparative health and prosperity: the career of Eugene O'Neill closely parallels that of Jeffers, and in the 1940's the two tragic writers often were damned together. Moreover, the critical superlatives which had been lavished upon Jeffers' poetry in the 1920's now began to cause reaction; his over-enthusiastic following had indeed begun to "praise him into obscurity." But perhaps the chief reason for the decline of Jeffers' reputation after 1935 was, quite simply, the decline in the quality of the long narrative poems published during the following decade.

When *Solstice and Other Poems* appeared in 1935, it was

reviewed without enthusiasm. Robert Penn Warren accurately described the title poem as "like nothing so much as an ether dream Jeffers might have about some of his own poetry." The narration was self-conscious, unconvincing, and lacking in the sense of immediacy characteristic of the best earlier narratives. Two years later *Such Counsels You Gave to Me* repeated the same pattern. And in 1941, *Be Angry at the Sun* included an astonishing short poem which confessed the author's dislike for his own title poem: "Tomorrow I will take up that heavy poem again / About Ferguson. . . ." As Stanley Kunitz remarked in reviewing the volume for *Poetry*: "It is old stuff to Jeffers; he is bored writing it, and, what is worse, we are permitted to sense his boredom, his feeling that he has spun too many myths out of himself." The poetic inspiration which had earlier created the characters of Tamar and Cawdor out of pure imagination had now become depleted. Although some of the new short poems achieved lyric beauty and philosophic insight, the decade from 1935 to 1945 did not add much to his poetic stature.

However, his popular reputation remained very great, and in 1938 Random House issued a large, handsome volume of *The Selected Poetry of Robinson Jeffers*. This included almost half of his poetic output to date, together with an interesting Foreword. The standards of selection for the poetry were, however, somewhat confused, as Jeffers himself admitted: *The Women at Point Sur* was omitted reluctantly, because it was "least understood and least liked"; "*Dear Judas* also was not liked and is therefore omitted." Otherwise, longer poems were selected partly on a basis of preference, partly of representativeness. Some of the most successful shorter poems were omitted for personal reasons. But despite omissions, the volume did collect the majority of his best poetry, and it was successful.

Meanwhile, in 1937, Jeffers visited Europe again, but without the stimulation resulting from his earlier visit. Then in 1941 he and his wife drove across the American continent to the East coast, where he had been invited to give a series of readings of his poetry. This trip turned into a kind of triumphal tour; the audiences which attended his readings bore witness to the continuing, tremendous popularity of the poet. In Cambridge, the Harvard authorities had assigned him a lecture room seating about four hundred; but the audience far exceeded capacity and late comers listened as best they could from the halls. For the full fifty minutes that he read from his poems, the overflow audience kept complete and fascinated silence.

During his tour of the eastern cities, Jeffers stopped at Camden to visit the house where Whitman had lived and to pay homage to the earlier poet. Although he had sometimes minimized Whitman's influence on his own poetry, he nevertheless felt a profound fellowship with him. And after his poetic reading in Cambridge, he paid unexpected homage to another contemporary American poet. I had driven him to Concord to visit the former home of Emerson and Thoreau, and we were returning toward Boston through the woods near Walden pond. Looking out at a tumble-down stone wall and the birch-trees beyond it, Jeffers suddenly exclaimed: "This is Robert Frost country."

During these years a series of critical essays and scholarly articles appearing in the literary magazines and quarterlies subjected Jeffers' poetry and philosophy to a more detailed analysis than had been hitherto possible. The excitement of literary discovery having faded, new questions—of ultimate value, and importance, and meaning—arose. Was the poetry as nihilistic as many believed, or did it express an acceptable philosophy of life? Did it describe clearly the current attitudes of materialistic science, or was it confused between a new materialism and an old romanticism? And did its prophetic denunciations warn against the now obvious dangers of fascism and world catastrophe, or did they contribute to the very evils they denounced? With a tragic depression fresh in the memory, and a second world war threatening from Europe, imagined horrors seemed unsalutary, and their psychological effect destructive. Timely criticism combined with scholarship to emphasize the dangers of the poetry, and both increasingly questioned its whole philosophy.

VIII *Involvement*

Meanwhile, Jeffers' new poetry of this period began to change its tone; by its conscious involvement in contemporary affairs, it seemed to negate the very premises of the earlier poetry. His 1941 volume began with a disturbing note: "I wish to lament the obsession with contemporary history that pins many of these pieces to the calendar, like butterflies to cardboard. Poetry . . . in general is the worse for being timely. . . . Yet it is right that a man's views be expressed, though the poetry should suffer for it."

By their author's own admission, these new poems suffered for being too much involved with the emotions of the day and for lacking perspective. Although his earlier elegy on "Woodrow Wilson" had been written from a perspective of eight years, a new poem entitled "Battle" was dated exactly: "(May 28, 1940)." What gives these new poems value is the imaginative structure of past prophecy to which they unconsciously refer. But their contemporaneity is compulsive, and the author apologizes for it.

The most interesting poem of this kind is "The Bowl of Blood," which attempts to present Adolf Hitler (called only "The Leader") as a character in tragic drama. It is narrated in the manner of Hardy's *Dynasts*, but its murky symbolism suggests Wagnerian opera. The two "Maskers" who introduce the piece emphasize the self-consciousness of the conception:

> *First Masker.* I do not know whether it is possible to
> present contemporary things in the shape of eternity.
> *Second.* If it were, it would please no one.

And the whole poem produces an effect of purposeful confusion, not—it must be admitted—inappropriate to its subject.

But the worst poem of this period is entitled "Shine, Empire." The title, of course, recalls the famous early poem, "Shine, Perishing Republic" and also the "Shine, Republic" of 1935. The three form a kind of trilogy, and they illustrate the changes in the author's poetic ideas over the years. The first conceived America as a republic in process of changing to empire; meanwhile the poet observed the change, but calmly kept his distance, knowing that "corruption / Never has been compulsory." The second described America as the inheritor of "the love of freedom [which] has been the quality of Western man. . . . a stubborn torch that flames from Marathon to Concord." And it directly exhorted the republic to "keep the tradition. . . . Be great, carve deep your heel marks." Now "Shine, Empire" bewails the historic actualization of what the first poem had prophesied, and against which the second had exhorted: America has become an empire, and the poet denounces the accomplished evil. From detached observation through ideal exhortation, the tone has changed to disturbed denunciation.

But what makes "Shine, Empire" a bad poem is not so much the author's "obsession with contemporary history" as the nature of it, and the personal irritation with which he expresses it:

Powerful and armed, neutral in the midst of madness,
  we might have held the whole world's balance
  and stood
Like a mountain in the wind. We were misled and took
  sides. We have chosen to share the crime and
  the punishment.
Perhaps justly, being part of Europe. Three thousand
  miles of ocean would hardly wash out the stains
Of all that mish-mash, blood, language, religion,
  snobbery. Three thousand miles in a ship would
  not make Americans.
I have often in weak moments thought of this people
  as something higher than the natural run of
  the earth.
I was quite wrong; we are lower.

First he defines imperialism, arbitrarily, as participation in alien wars. Second he indulges in name-calling ("all that mish-mash"). And finally he condemns his own idealism as delusion, without recognizing that the real fault of this idealism is that it refuses to accept the patterns of history. "Shine, Perishing Republic" had achieved excellence because of its clear recognition that these patterns often negate the idealisms of humanity. But "Shine, Empire" now takes sides, and it blindly rejects the poet's own earlier insight.

The extreme obloquy and criticism which Jeffers and his poetry suffered during the 1940's was caused partly by the badness of many of these new poems and partly by the unpopularity of the political opinions which he insisted in expressing in them. Personal isolationism had always been a central tenet of his philosophy. But gradually over the years his own personal isolation from the "perishing republic" had changed to an emotional involvement in it. Following his family's move to California he had always identified himself with the "West," and in his mind "America" had become "West." Looking back at his country from Ireland in 1930, he praised it for this reason. All his poetic life had been lived "West of the West," and now he idealized the American "West" also. But by a bitter paradox of history, the national isolationism which Jeffers began to idealize in the 1930's was even then in process of becoming unpopular and obsolete. And as World War II engulfed America, it came to seem almost treasonous.

During World War II Jeffers continued to write short pieces repeating his denunciation of America's intervention and his disgust at what he considered the hypocrisy of her leaders:

> The squid, frightened and angry, shoots darkness
> Out of her ink-sac; the fighting destroyer throws
>   out a smoke-screen;
> And fighting governments produce lies.

Unpublished for obvious reasons during the war, these poems were collected in book form, together with a long title poem, *The Double-Axe*, in 1948. But the poet's opinions were so extreme, and his assertion of them so controversial, that the publishers introduced the volume with a note: "Random House feels compelled to go on record with its disagreement over some of the political views pronounced by the poet in this volume." Rare in the history of literature, this kind of publisher's note served to underline the quarrel between the poet and his public which had gradually been intensifying during the last fifteen years. By 1948 Jeffers' reputation had reached its lowest point.

IX *Medea*

But, meanwhile, he had been writing other things which would prove more successful and popular. He had long been an admirer of the tragic actress, Judith Anderson, and in 1941 she appeared in a production by a theatre group in Carmel of "The Tower Beyond Tragedy." The success of this production and the urging of Miss Anderson then led him to attempt a free adaptation of the *Medea* of Euripides for professional production. After the war in 1946, this new *Medea* was published. If the reviews of the book were somewhat mixed, the notices of the dramatic production which followed were uniformly enthusiastic.

On October 20, 1947, Jeffers' *Medea* was produced on Broadway, with Judith Anderson in the title role. Led by Brooks Atkinson, the New York critics joined in acclaiming the play for both the acting and its conception. It ran continuously for 214 performances, closing on May 15, 1948 at the end of the regular Broadway season. And the next September it opened in San Francisco, again with Miss Anderson in the title role. On September 5, 1948, Jeffers published in the *San Francisco Chronicle*, a long prose Preface to the play in which he explained his attitudes toward it and related it to contemporary history by means of interesting parallels.

The great age of Greek drama, he wrote, "began in a time of exultation when the great defensive war with Persia was triumphantly concluded." But after the period of Aeschylus and Sophocles, an exhausting civil war with Sparta caused a shift in the Greek mood. By the time of Euripides the world had changed, and "the great dream was fading." The plays of Euripides reflected this period of disillusionment, and substituted a new "intensity and fury" for the old "sublimity" of Aeschylus and the old "nobility" of Sophocles. To Jeffers this disillusioned "intensity and fury" seemed both congenial and appropriate to the modern times.

But long before his adaptation of Euripides' play the myth of Medea had appealed to the poet. In "Solstice" he had attempted, unsuccessfully, to naturalize it in a modern narrative. And the ambivalent mixture of love and hate felt by Medea toward her husband and children continued to fascinate him. His own ambivalent feeling toward his country and toward the poems which he was writing out of his love and hate for it seemed similar in its psychology. In *Solstice*, a short poem entitled "Love the Wild Swan" had expressed this ambivalence: " 'I hate my verses, every line, every word.' "—But, he warned himself, there is the objective beauty of "the wild swan" to be loved, beyond the poet's subjective involvement in the tragedies of contemporary history.

X *The Final Phase*

Throughout his life Jeffers had struggled to understand and to describe the universal problem of involvement and isolation— of society and solitude. His early poetry had succeeded to a remarkable degree in suggesting objectively the tragic emotions of involvement through the techniques of myth and of prophecy. But his later poetry tended to naturalize myth in the form of contemporary realism and to abandon prophecy for simple exhortation and denunciation. Therefore, his later poetry became sharply divided—the narratives became more realistic; the poems of idea and interpretation became more intellectual. And this new dichotomy found its clearest expression in the title poem of *The Double-Axe*.

In 1948 *The Double-Axe* was poorly received, and has remained largely unpopular. But the poem did succeed in describing clearly and dramatically its author's ideas. And its form and technique emphasized the dichotomy of these poetic ideas. The title poem actually consists of two separate poems of two different types. The first retells once again the violent type of story which all his narratives have told in one form or another, but this time the telling is of unusual starkness. Then the second poem dramatizes the inner conflicts of an old man who is struggling to understand and to reconcile himself to the events. The first poem, entitled significantly "The Love and the Hate," expresses an ambivalence in which the two emotions are inextricably mixed. But the second, entitled "The Inhumanist," gropes toward the expression of the non-humanistic philosophy which transcends the human involvement in both love and hate.

Meanwhile two earlier dramatic poems by Jeffers were being produced on Broadway. On October 5, 1947, *Dear Judas* was presented at the Mansfield Theatre in New York in an adaptation by Michael Myerberg. The play ran for only sixteen performances, but it attracted considerable critical attention. Brooks Atkinson praised its poetic intensity, while admitting its lack of dramatic movement. But George Jean Nathan, who found it dull, complained that it was too "declamatory and sanctimonious." That this most revolutionary conception of the gospel story could be described as sanctimonious suggests that Jeffers' anti-orthodox interpretation of Christianity may be more deeply religious than most critics have thought.

Following the long, successful run of *Medea*, Judith Anderson persuaded the American National Theatre and Academy to produce *The Tower Beyond Tragedy* at the "ANTA" playhouse in New York. On November 26, 1950, the play opened with Miss Anderson in the role of Clytemnestra, as she had been in the amateur production in Carmel nine years before. When several of the New York critics expressed enthusiasm, there seemed hope for a successful run. But again the poetic narrative lacked the dramatic values necessary for theatrical success; after thirty-two performances, the play closed.

During the early 1940's Jeffers had allowed himself to become involved in the political passions of the time, and his poetry had suffered from it. During the late 1940's he had observed a resurgence of interest in his dramatic poetry, but he had not allowed himself to become involved in its success or failure. Meanwhile he had kept a remarkably objective attitude toward his greatest "involvement" of all—that with his wife. Throughout his life he had written poems to her and about her. In 1941, even when denouncing the politics of the time from a strongly partisan bias, he had imagined calmly the mortal fate of the human being he loved most. And in the short poem "For Una" he distilled the essence of the emotion which transcends involvement:

> I built her a tower when I was young—
> Sometime she will die—
> I built it with my hands, I hung
> Stones in the sky.

> Old but still strong I climb the stone—
> Sometime she will die—
> Climb the steep rough steps alone,
> And weep in the sky.

In 1948 Robinson and Una Jeffers visited Europe for the last time together, then returned to Carmel. There, in 1950, Una Jeffers died. She had been older than her husband and he had prepared himself for the event, yet it seemed almost to mark also the end of his life. After her death he continued to live in "Tor House" with his son Donnan and the grandchildren. But all his later poems seem written in the memory of Una Jeffers and their life together.

In 1954 Jeffers' last volume, *Hungerfield and Other Poems,* was published, The title poem both begins and ends with a direct address to his wife's memory and with a poetic recall of her death. Between these realities, the narrative poem imagines the myth of "Hungerfield," a contemporary Hercules who wrestled with death for the life of his mother, "Alcmena Hungerfield," and *won,* only to regret bitterly his overweening pride. This strangely supernatural story counterpoints the emotions of the poet at the memory of his wife's death, and it leads to the final reconciliation with it:

> Here is the poem, dearest; you will never read it
>   nor hear it. You were more beautiful
> Than a hawk flying; you were faithful and a lion heart
>   like this rough hero Hungerfield. But the ashes have
>   fallen

And the flame has gone up; nothing human remains. You
 are earth and air; you are the beauty of the ocean
And the great streaming triumphs of sundown; you are
 alive and well in the tender young grass rejoicing
When soft rain falls all night, and little rosy-fleeced
 clouds float on the dawn. —I shall be with you
 presently.

But between these personal poems, the bulk of the final volume is taken up with "The Cretan Woman," a free adaptation of the *Hippolytus* of Euripides. Jeffers had suggested this play in his Preface to *Medea*, recalling that "Euripides was hissed off the stage for showing a real woman desperately in love; his first 'Phaedra.'" And now he adapted the play for modern readers, as he had *Medea*, but with less success, for he now kept the character of "Aphrodite" as an actual stage presence. The play was acted in New York by a theatre group off Broadway, but the production was not successful.

From 1954 until his death in January, 1962, Jeffers continued to live quietly in Carmel, writing very little. But during these years his critical reputation has recovered somewhat from its nadir during the World War II. Articles about him have begun appearing more frequently in the recent periodicals—including several in foreign languages. In 1955 a complete catalogue of the Robinson Jeffers Collection at Occidental College was published under separate cover. In 1956 Radcliffe Squires published *The Loyalties of Robinson Jeffers*, the first book-length critical study in twenty years. In 1958 Jeffers was awarded the Academy of American Poets' Fellowship for "distinguished poetic achievement." In 1958 also, Mercedes Monjian's interpretation of his poetic ideas appeared, subtitled "A Study in Inhumanism." And in 1959 *The American Book Collector* featured two articles praising his poetry and listing an imposing bibliography of recent critical works dealing with it.

Considered historically, Jeffers remains one of the most important poets of the years before the great depression. But in the last quarter of a century his reputation has fluctuated not only with the events and tastes of the times but with the changing tone and quality of his own successive poems. Always a few readers—including some major poets and critics—have considered his work of the greatest permanent value. Always other readers —including many major critics—have considered it beneath notice.

Few authors in the history of literature have excited greater differences of opinion; and few have seen their reputations change so greatly in their own lifetimes. But critical praise and blame affected Jeffers himself very little. From his isolated rock tower he continued to gaze southward at the wild promontories of the coast and westward at the far horizons of the ocean, rather than eastward at his fellow men. He never, of course, achieved the ideal indifference which he imagined for Orestes:

> But young or old, few years of many,
> signified less than nothing
> To him who had climbed the tower beyond time,
> consciously, and cast humanity. . .

Both his poetry and his reputation might have fared better if he had held closer to this ideal. Meanwhile, his poetry awaits the gradual verdict of posterity. And the problems which it poses seem all the more interesting because of their difficulty and their uncertainty.

CHAPTER 2

The Poetry of Myth:
The Long Poems

ANYONE ATTEMPTING to describe, to analyze, to criticize, and to judge the poems of Robinson Jeffers is faced with difficult problems: In what terms are these poems to be described? By what logic are they to be analyzed? By what standards are they to be criticized? By what laws are they to be judged? Jeffers himself has suggested that the primary virtue of his poems lies in their "singularity," or uniqueness. But neither he nor his critics have been able to define this singularity.

Certainly his poems do not fit into any of the usual categories of literary criticism. His long poems are sometimes narrative, sometimes dramatic, sometimes philosophic; they are usually a mixture of all three. His short poems are sometimes lyric, sometimes philosophic, sometimes personal, but seldom conventional. The only quality that can be affirmed of them all is that they are Jeffersian—few could have been written by any other poet. But what constitutes their uniqueness, and, occasionally, their excellence?

Most critics—even most sympathetic critics—have simply emphasized the qualities which Jeffers' poetry lacks. The long poems, for instance, have usually been called tragic, and have been condemned for lacking the virtues of classical tragedy. Or they have been called narrative, and have been denounced for lacking the fully developed and individualized characters which a novelist should create. Or when they have dealt with the materials of Greek mythology, they have been censured for not being "Hellenic." By the standards of Aeschylus, of Aristotle, or even of William Faulkner, these poems have seemed to fail.

Not only have critics condemned Jeffers' poems for not measuring up to traditional standards, but they have praised some and criticized others for contradictory reasons. Very few readers have agreed on the pre-eminence of any one of his long poems. Each of the following has been chosen as Jeffers' "best" by some critic of repute: "Tamar," "Roan Stallion," "The Tower Beyond Tragedy," "Cawdor," "Dear Judas," "The Loving Shepherdess," "Thurso's Landing," "Give Your Heart to the Hawks," "At the Birth of an Age," "The Double Axe," and "Hungerfield." But each of these has also been judged unsuccessful by others of these same critics for one reason or another.

In the course of his long career, Jeffers himself has gradually approached the definition of his philosophy, which he has named "inhumanism." His recent critics have focused upon this— Radcliffe Squires has praised "The Double Axe" because it best illustrates this philosophic idea. But the clear expression of an idea seldom qualifies any poem for greatness. And Jeffers' first mature poem, "Tamar," had mostly been innocent of ideas; the reasons and the interpretations came later. The unique quality of his poetry does not lie primarily in its philosophy, although "inhumanism" is a singular enough idea. Its uniqueness—and whatever of excellence it may possess—lies rather in its emotional conception and in its poetic expression.

In the beginning, with the publication of "Tamar" and "Roan Stallion," Jeffers burst upon the reading public with an almost explosive force. These strange poems seemed literally to shock readers into attention and to compel an admiration like that felt for the forces of nature. And, in fact, the protagonists of these poems resembled forces of nature rather than individual human beings. Tamar and California were as non-human as the Greek Europa and Pasiphäe; rather than realistic fictions, they acted out modern myths.

The concept of myth may help to describe and to explain the uniqueness of Jeffers' long poems. For a true myth is "an imaginary story usually concerning deities and demi-gods." The characters of true myth are never fully rounded human beings but primarily personifications of natural forces. In their first conception they are not the complex protagonists of classical tragedy, doomed to failure by some human fault—they are single-souled gods or demigods. They are superhuman or subhuman but not the human heroes of the later tragedies, or the individualized characters of modern novels.

Because these characters of ancient myth were primarily

forces of nature, they were not bound by the laws of civilization. They had very little to do with morality: they were not immoral, but pre-moral. The mythical incest of Coelus and Terra was simply the meeting of heaven and earth—when Melville expressed horror at this ancient story, he was imagining it in modern, moral terms; and the modern incest of "Tamar" was similarly imagined. Jeffers first created his mythical character in terms of natural compulsion, but he then modified it in terms of civilized morality. Tamar (like California) acted with all the single-minded amorality of a character in ancient myth, but her acts took place in the modern world. And this caused confusion.

Every modern writer of myth faces this problem: his characters cannot be moral, because they are primarily demigods motivated by those natural forces of primitive life which prevailed before morality was codified and which eternally exist. But his mythical characters also live in the modern world, with whose moral codes they feel themselves in conflict. Even if they are imagined back into the world of classical myth—as in "The Tower Beyond Tragedy"—their psychology remains modern. The mythical characters of the modern poet, therefore, find themselves in conflict with modern civilization. And their author must somehow mediate this conflict, remembering not only the demand of his primitive characters that their inner nature be given full expression, but also that of his modern readers that moral law must prevail.

Conceived in terms of myth—rather than of tragedy, or of fiction, or of philosophy—Jeffers' long poems can be described and judged by their own "singular" virtues or faults, rather than by the lack of virtues to which they never pretended. The particular qualities of his individual poems appear clearly when described in these terms, and the separate poems fall into definable groups. The changes of form and psychology which have marked his creative career assume a meaningful pattern. If these changes in his poetic conceptions were not always for the good, at least they were not capricious, but were directed by the logic (or the illogic) of modern myth.

I *The Four Periods*

Jeffers' career falls into four periods during which he developed different attitudes toward his mythical materials. His long poems fall into four groups, or types, roughly corresponding to these periods. During the first, from 1925 to 1929, Jeffers conceived his long poems almost purely as modern myths. During the second, from 1928 to 1935, his myths changed to resemble realistic fictions. During the third period, from 1935 to 1948, his myths became self-conscious, and he changed them to resemble case histories of abnormal psychology. And during the final period, his myths became frankly supernatural and ideal.

Jeffers' first period was one of intense poetic activity, during which he published the poems which made him famous: "Tamar," "Roan Stallion," and "The Tower Beyond Tragedy." In these modern myths, the characters, creations of the pure imagination, responded to psychological compulsions more powerful than they. In creating them Jeffers was guided entirely by his own poetic motives, because he was writing before fame had forced public responsibility on him. Only after criticism led him to re-examine his motives did he seek to rationalize and to justify them.

Following this first period of pure creation—and continuous with it—came a transitional phase during which Jeffers sought to clarify and to explain his (mostly unconscious) motives. The mental turmoil which accompanied this effort is reflected in the poetic intensity and the psychological confusion of "The Women at Point Sur." During this time he also wrote long letters to his friends and critics describing in detail his "intentions." And at the end of this transitional period he composed the more conscious myths of "Dear Judas" and "The Loving Shepherdess:"

His second period was ushered in by "Cawdor," in 1928. This poem, together with "Thurso's Landing" and "Give Your Heart to the Hawks," departed in significant ways from the earlier patterns of pure myth. The setting was uniformly localized on the coast south of Carmel and was described in more realistic detail. The characters became less single-minded, less compulsive, and more recognizable as complex human beings. The plot lengthened, and the episodes multiplied until the long poem came to approximate the short novel. In other words, myth moved in the direction of modern, realistic fiction. The characters, although still abnormal, became more moral, and sometimes even achieved a measure of heroism. Therefore, the long poems of this second period usually pleased the readers who had criticized the earlier myths for their excess of violence and immorality.

Jeffers' third period began with the publication of "Solstice"—a brief but turgid retelling of the Medea story in a California setting. But what differentiated this poem—and the succeeding "Mara" and "Such Counsels You Gave to Me" from the earlier myths, was progressive lack of conviction. The protagonists no longer felt themselves compelled by inner, natural forces; rather they recognized themselves as sick, and their motives as distorted. Their author's point of view had shifted from natural myth to civilized psychoanalysis. And because he no longer believed in his characters, they no longer believed in themselves. The tone of these poems shifted from the major confidence of "Roan Stallion" to the self-conscious decadence of the minor tales of Poe, but without Poe's technical excellence. And no one liked these long poems of the third period—not even their author.

During this unsuccessful period, beginning with "At the Birth of an Age" in the *Solstice* volume, Jeffers seemed to be groping toward the formulation of the idealized myth, or supernatural fable. Beginning with the narration of a Norse myth, "At the Birth of an Age" gradually developed into a poetic debate over the ideal problems suggested by the myth. Later "The Double Axe" developed this same technique, beginning with a brief realistic narrative of "The Love and the Hate" and concluding with an imagined debate about the conflicts involved. In his fourth period, Jeffers was gradually changing from myth-maker to philosophic poet. And with his final long poem, "Hungerfield," he turned to a frank supernaturalism which rivaled the psychological horrors of Poe but also remembered the multiple meanings of ancient myth.

II "Tamar"

First of the many long poems which Jeffers published during the course of his long career was "Tamar"; for although his early *Californians* had included a group of short narrative poems, none had been fully developed. "Tamar" was his first poem to achieve fame, and for it he first claimed the virtue of "singularity." After thirty-eight years "Tamar" still remains the most "singular" of his poems, and one of the strangest in literature. Some critics have considered it his best; others have dismissed it with a variety of epithets. Both historically and critically, therefore, "Tamar" seems of primary importance: the problems it suggests are crucial both for the interpretation of Jeffers and for the criticism of literature.

Those critics who have valued "Tamar" least usually have begun with a simple summary of the plot. Thus summarized, the poem seems absurd. The chief difference between poetry and prose is the difference between affective expression and factual statement, and the facts of Tamar's biography are neither prosaic nor amenable to statement in prose.

The plot which the poem "Tamar" narrates in poetic language is essentially that of the oldest of Greek myths. It was first described in American literature by Melville's *Pierre, or the Ambiguities.* At the end of this unsuccessful novel, Melville explained: "Old Titan's self was the son of incestuous Coelus and Terra, the son of incestuous Heaven and Earth. And Titan married his mother Terra, another and accumulatively incestuous match. And thereof Enceladus was one issue. So Enceladus was both the son and grandson of an incest." This mytho-poetic lineage, with only a change of name and gender, also describes Jeffers' Tamar. The plot of the poem retells an ancient and archetypal myth, and although the narrative of the action is realistic, the name, the structure, and the poetic overtones are purely mythical. "Tamar" may be described as a modern myth about myth.

This doubly mythical quality is constantly emphasized. The name recalls a biblical incest first chronicled in II Samuel, chapter 13. And at the beginning of the poem this name is emphasized: "His sister Tamar / Was with him, and his mind ran on her name." Later Tamar learns of her father's incest from the spirit-voice of Aunt Stella, who comforts her: "a trap so baited / Was laid to catch you when the world began, / Before the granite foundation." And at the end Tamar explains to her father:

> ". . . time stands still old man, you'll learn when
> you have lived at the muddy root
> Under the rock of things; all times are now, to-day
> plays on last year and the inch of our future
> Made the first morning of the world. You named me for
> the monument in a desolate graveyard,
> Fool, and I say you were deceived, it was out of me
> that fire lit you and your Helen, your body
> Joined with your sister's
> Only because I was to be named Tamar and to love my
> brother and my father.
> I am the fountain."

This timelessness of myth is emphasized most effectively by the structure of the poem. In terms of action, the poem moves steadily through conflict to catastrophe. But in terms of meaning, it moves steadily through discovery to understanding.

"Tamar" begins with a minor action, succeeded by presentiment and dream. Then follows the narrative of the incest of Tamar with her brother. But then comes a purely unrealistic episode in which Aunt Stella, "lying blank-eyed in the dark, egged on her dreams of vision," revealing to Tamar the earlier incest of her father with his sister Helen; and this long vista of ancestral horror, uniting the present with the past, gives the poem mythical depth. The next episode narrates the only "normal" action of the poem—the one in which Tamar seduces Will Andrews in order to cover up her love for her brother. But then follows the strangest episode of all, combining factual narrative with pure unrealism. After experiencing and recognizing her family's degradation, Tamar performs an obscene dance at nightfall on the tideline and symbolically suffers violation from the ghosts of all those Indian tribes whom her ancestors had killed and from whom they had wrested this land. The next-to-last episode tells of the psychological incest of daughter with father—completing the circle—and the final episode culminates with the utter destruction of "the house," and all those in it.

Structurally, then, the two central episodes of "Tamar" describe first, the vision of ancestral evil; and second, the symbolic, ritual dance by which Tamar seeks to exorcise this ancestral evil. Between these two, Jeffers introduced his poetic Invocation: "O blower of music through the crooked bugles." Finally, as if to emphasize the central meaning of the strangest episode, Jeffers chose Tamar's ritual dance for an anthology entitled *This Is My Best*, edited by Whit Burnett. The most unrealistic and incredible of all the episodes of this most strange poem seemed to its author, many years later, his "best" poetry.

Moreover, in this central section of "Tamar" Jeffers specifically asserted the basic morality of his myth—an assertion which he was to qualify in later years. His "blower of music through the crooked bugles" specifically welcomed Tamar, along with the other forces of nature:

> God who makes beauty
> Disdains no creature, nor despised that wounded
> Tired and betrayed body. She in the starlight

> And little noises of the rising tide
> Naked and not ashamed bore a third part
> With the ocean and keen stars in the consistence
> And dignity of the world.

And on the next page the ghost of Tamar's mother praised her:

> You called me, you have more hot and blind, wild-blooded
> And passionate life than any other creature.
> How could I ever leave you while the life lasts?
> God pity us both, a cataract life
> Dashing itself to pieces in an instant.

These poetic affirmations suggest the crucial problem of "Tamar," and of all Jeffers' poetic myths. How can the character who most completely embodies the ancestral evil of humanity be welcomed wholeheartedly by the God who makes beauty? How can she be described as having "more wild-blooded life than any other creature?" This question, repeated by many critics after the publication of "Tamar," and formulated in many different ways, was to trouble Jeffers throughout his career. Writing to James Rorty about 1928, he declared: "Tamar seemed to my later thought to have a tendency to romanticize unmoral freedom, and it was evident that a good many people took it that way. That way lies destruction of course, often for the individual but always for the social organism." As the years went on, his characters tended increasingly not only to recognize their own immorality but to suffer diminution from it. Jeffers progressively seemed to deny his characters that full-blooded life which made Tamar so memorable. Only once, in his "Apology for Bad Dreams," did he reaffirm his earlier belief in Tamar:

> Imagined victims our salvation: white as the half moon
>   at midnight
> Someone flamelike passed me, saying, "I am Tamar Cauldwell,
>   I have my desire."

The problem of literary morality which "Tamar" poses is fundamental. But it is not simple: no single answer is possible. In one sense, "Tamar" is an immoral poem; in another sense, a deeply moral one. "Tamar" could suggest to Professor Winters the sarcastic moral: "My impulse to commit incest may horrify you; your impulse to commit murder and arson may horrify me; but we should ignore each other and proceed."[1] But "Tamar"

could also seem to Benjamin de Casseres "a perfect work of art."
Even a theoretically dispassionate analyst cannot prove one
judgment true, the other false. The poem is profoundly—and
inevitably—ambivalent. Near the beginning of "Tamar" the author
asks:

> . . . Was it the wild rock coast
> Of her breeding, . . .
> . . . the earth-ending water
> That moves all the west taught her this freedom?

And he lectures his heroine:

> . . . Ah, Tamar,
> It was not good, not wise, not safe, not provident,
> Not even, for custom creates nature, natural,
> Though all other license were . . .

But near the end of his poem he scornfully ridicules Tamar's
weak brother:

> And then he would look at the bed and stiffen
> In a brittle rage, feel with thrust under-lip
> Virtuous, an outcrop of morality in him
> To grow ridiculous and wish to be cruel . . .

The fundamental conflict which both creates and destroys
"Tamar" is the conflict between the forces of inhuman nature
and those of human morality. Stated in terms of myth, the
conflict lies between demigod and man. Tamar is in one sense
a demigod—the doubly incestuous, mythical offspring of tyrant
father and earth mother. But she is in another sense a human
being living in the modern world where "custom has created
nature," and she therefore seems unnatural. The ambivalence is
inevitable: the poet can only describe it, and seek to suggest an
understanding of it.

The final sections of the poem do clearly describe Tamar's
single-mined devotion to her inner nature, seemingly so unnatural. She emerges in the end an integrated human being
whose poetic value lies in her absolute integrity. To poor, normal
Will Andrews she explains: "you are not hard enough . . . only
stone or fire / Should marry into this house." But Tamar herself
becomes the perfect embodiment of human evil, who both accepts and welcomes her fate.

It must be admitted, however, that earlier sections of the poem sometimes tend to "romanticize unmoral freedom." Jeffers did not succeed completely in freeing his heroine's unmoral freedom from the taint of romantic sentimentality. To be sure, he never implied that the impulse to commit incest, murder, or arson was good; and his poetry always described the disasters resulting from these evils. But there remains in "Tamar" a trace of the sickly-sweet sentimentality of some of his earlier poems— such as "Fauna" (whose title again emphasizes its mytho-poetic intention). Jeffers consciously recognized this romantic element and sought to discipline it in his later poems.

The problem of modern myth which the author of a poem like "Tamar" must solve, is probably insoluble in terms of traditional western and Christian morality. Any character who embodies absolute evil, and who utterly rejects human morality and human society, cannot be described sympathetically as full of life and beauty without casting doubt on the justice of this morality and society. Any absolute devil—any human incarnation of the purely destructive power of nature—cannot be described as purely beautiful, because traditional Christianity has conceived of God as purely good. Only Oriental religions have incarnated the purely destructive power of nature in gods like Shiva, and his wives Kali and Durga. Abstractly, Emerson described the idea in "Brahma," and Whitman suggested the inclusion of this diabolic power in the godhead in his poem "Chanting the Square Deific." But when the modern poet seeks to imagine a female devil for his realistic myth, he must either describe her as evil or be accused of romantic diabolism.

What makes the problem of "Tamar" so extreme is that the story is imagined realistically in modern terms, yet Tamar's nature is described mythically as absolutely evil. In "The Tower Beyond Tragedy" Jeffers returned to antique mythology, and avoided the issue of modern realism. In "Roan Stallion" he described his heroine's love for the stallion as psychological only—and therefore as not unnatural—and her crime as human also. In "Dear Judas" he suggested a modern interpretation of the biblical story in terms of secular psychology and history. But in "Tamar" he sought to naturalize antique, inhuman myth in purely modern, human terms. If he failed to achieve the impossible, his relative success seems the more remarkable.

This success is emphasized by the subsequent development in Eugene O'Neill's more realistic dramas of two themes which "Tamar" had embodied in mythical terms. As Jeffers' poem approaches its climax, Tamar exclaims three times over having "my three lovers / Here in one room. . . .How can I help being happy?" And this theme of Tamar's love for brother, father, and lover, was dramatized in psychological terms in O'Neill's *Strange Interlude*, whose heroine also repeatedly exclaimed over "my three lovers," psychologically resembling brother, father, and lover. Following this, O'Neill's greatest play, *Mourning Becomes Electra*, created a new heroine whose intellectual recognition of her evil and incestuous nature paralleled Tamar's more active recognition of the same evil.

Any final critical judgment of "Tamar" must be mixed. Certainly it is one of the most singular poems in literature. Probably it remains, in George Sterling's words, "among the unforgettable dreams of art." But to most readers the theme of incest which it treats realistically does not seem fitted for such treatment. Therefore, the poem properly deserves the critical adjectives "lurid" and "surcharged." But the poem is not "formless" (as some have held), and it is not truly "neurotic." Its form includes a mixture of realistic action and unrealistic vision, but these are alternated with conscious intent to suggest the meanings of myth and the images of dream. The poem is not neurotic in the sense that Jeffers' later narratives are: the heroine is a single-minded and integrated being who both recognizes and accepts the evil of her own nature. Probably no poet will ever attempt another "Tamar." But if the poem had never been written, our literature would be the poorer for it.

An earlier and shorter narrative poem, "The Coast-Range Christ," was also published in the "Tamar" volume. Less singular and less successful, this poem remains remarkable for several reasons. The long and irregular but sometimes monotonously rhymed couplets illustrate the poet's transitional experiments with verse: they are interesting, but contrast sharply with the wholly original and skilfully modulated versification of "Tamar." The poem's form is interesting also in that it combines realistic narrative with poetic interpretation of the action: although the narrative remains somewhat pedestrian, the concluding strophes and antistrophes of choros and antichoros seem, by contrast, to take wings and soar. And finally these poetic strophes suggest for the first time the challenging interpretations of the Christian myth which Jeffers was to embody more completely in "Dear Judas."

III   *"Roan Stallion"*

When *Tamar and Other Poems* was reprinted by a major publishing house, it was added to a group of new poems, including "Roan Stallion" and "The Tower Beyond Tragedy." But "Roan Stallion" was printed first, and was named first in the title of the combined volume. This fact emphasizes the importance of the poem in the eyes of both author and publisher. Add to this the brevity of the poem—it is the shortest of all Jeffers' major narratives—and "Roan Stallion" assumes major significance. Since its publication in 1925, readers and critics have agreed that it is one of Jeffers' best.

"Roan Stallion" contrasts with "Tamar" in almost every way. Both poems are consciously mythical, and both myths are naturalized on the California coast. But "Roan Stallion" is brief and concentrated, where "Tamar" is long and diffuse; it is unified in form and action, but "Tamar" is episodic; it realizes its myth through normal and psychological action, rather than the abnormal and unnatural; and it interprets its story by means of symbols and ideas, rather than by visions and dark sayings.

The myth of "Roan Stallion" is perhaps the commonest and most persistent of all ancient myths: the legendary love of a man or a woman for a beast, which produced most of the gods of Egypt and many of the demigods of Greece. The myth of Pasiphäe, whose passion for a bull created the monstruous minotaur, is most notorious. The myth of Europa, who was carried away by Zeus in the form of a bull, probably suggested the naming of the heroine of "Roan Stallion" California. But Jeffers himself has recalled the myth of Leda and the swan; and the title of his later lyric, "Love the Wild Swan," recalls the same myth. If the wild swan symbolizes the beauty of the natural world, the roan stallion symbolizes the power of it. The love of California for the roan stallion therefore naturally suggests Jeffers' idea of "breaking out of humanity" to a love of nature in all its aspects.

"Roan Stallion"—even more than most of Jeffers' narrative poems—is, by its author's conscious intention, pure myth. This fact is emphasized by a central passage of the poem:

> The fire threw up figures
> And symbols meanwhile, racial myths formed and dissolved
>   in it, the phantom rulers of humanity
> That without being are yet more real than what they are
>   born of, and without shape, shape that which makes them:
> The nerves and the flesh go by shadowlike, the limbs
>   and the lives shadowlike, these shadows remain,
>   these shadows
> To whom temples, 'to whom churches, to whom labors and
>   wars, visions and dreams are dedicate:

The poem is a racial myth. But more than this, "Roan Stallion" is also a myth of the American West. The heroine is named California, and she is described as one quarter Spanish, one quarter Indian, and one half Anglo-Saxon. Married to a degenerate who has been "shriveled with bad living" and alienated from him, she admires the wild stallion which he has won by gambling and keeps in his corral. "She thought, if he could range in freedom, / Shaking the red-roan mane for a flag on the bare hills." One night by moonlight she rides him to the hilltop, and imagines: "O clean power!" But neither the animal power nor the human California is free. The next night she flees from her husband to the corral of the stallion, where he follows her, to be trampled to death. But "then California moved by some obscure human fidelity / Lifted the rifle," and shot the stallion. "She turned then on her little daughter the mask of a woman / Who has killed God." Unlike Tamar, who follows her lawless nature to a wild end, California accepts the limits of the human condition. And the poem rejects the romantically possible ending in which the wild heroine and her stallion might have escaped from human society to run wild in a wild West.

"Roan Stallion" differs from "Tamar" not only in the nature of its heroine and her story but also in the manner of its telling. Where "Tamar" narrated a story of physical action in explicit terms, "Roan Stallion" describes action largely in symbolic and psychological ones. It consists of three major episodes, of which only the final is physically important. The techniques of symbolic narration and psychological implication are characteristic of Jeffers at his best.

The first major episode tells of California's journey to town on Christmas Eve to buy presents for her little daughter, whom her husband has forgotten. Her motives are simple and natural. On her return journey she is forced to ford a stream swollen by flash floods: the incident seems unimportant, but it symbolically develops the theme. As the mare trembles in the stream, California imagines the identity of the power of the swollen water with the power of the wild stallion. When the mare retreats in panic, California abandons the buggy to ride the mare through the water, suggesting her own psychological identity with the mare. And their immersion in the torrent symbolizes her baptism into the religion of nature, in which the stains of her earlier life with her renegade husband are washed clean.

The second major episode tells of California's ride on the stallion by moonlight to the hilltop, where she prostrates herself under his hooves. This episode is much simpler than the first, but it gains complexity of meaning through the repeated use of a single simile—the woman's head under the animal's hooves seems like a stone:

> The small dark head under his nostrils: a small round
>   stone, that smelt human, black hair growing from it:
> The skull shut the light in: it was not possible for
>   any eyes
> To know what throbbed and shone under the sutures of
>   the skull, or a shell full of lightning
> Had scared the roan strength, and he'd have broken
>   tether, screaming, and run for the valley.

The simile emphasizes, realistically, the outer similarity of skull and stone to the animal, but the immense inner difference of the "shell full of lightning." It suggests the further identity of skull and stone in their ultimate physical nature—a fact emphasized by the poet's apostrophe to "The atom bounds-breaking." Finally, the simile suggests the psychological origin of the myth itself: "Out of the fire in the small round stone that black moss covered." The outer action is negligible, but the inner action has been magnified, both in its intensity and in its significance.

Finally, "Roan Stallion" suggests for the first time Jeffers' central philosophic idea, later named "inhumanism."

> Humanity is the start of the race; I say
> Humanity is the mold to break away from, the crust to
>   break through, the coal to break into fire,
> The atom to be split.

But this poem emphasizes (as the later poems sometimes do not) the human origins and values of this supposedly inhuman idea. In "Roan Stallion" the versification twice accents the word humanity. When humanity suffers and learns through tragedy— "Tragedy that breaks man's face and a white fire flies out of it;" —then man achieves nobility. Human nature is the start of the race: California's love for her child started her on her tragic journey, both physically and psychologically. The poem achieves a complete integration of the idea with the tragic narrative.

IV *"The Tower Beyond Tragedy"*

"The Tower Beyond Tragedy," the third long poem in Jeffers' first major volume, is very different from the other two, but has proved even more successful. It abandons the California coast of the present to return to the Mycenae of ancient Greek myth. However, it modifies the myth for modern purposes, and Jeffers progressively develops a poetic idea alien to Greek thought. More than in "Tamar" or "Roan Stallion," Jeffers in "The Tower" achieves effects through poetic rather than realistic devices. Therefore, it has been criticized by different writers as not being "Hellenic," nor realistic, and ending in a "confusion of mystical philosophy." Nevertheless, "The Tower Beyond Tragedy" has always been one of the most popular of Jeffers' long poems: Mark Van Doren called it "undoubtedly one of the great American poems," and George Sterling considered it Jeffers' "best." But because two of Jeffers' chief critics, Powell and Squires, have not cared for it, little has been written to explain its complexity.

On the surface level, "The Tower Beyond Tragedy" retells the myth of Electra and Orestes, and two early versions bore the titles "The New Oresteia" and "The Last Oresteia." But a third version was entitled "Beyond Tragedy," and the final one emphasized the symbolic "Tower" to whose inner security both Jeffers and his ideal Orestes attained. Structurally also the poem progresses from ancient myth to modern idea. The first section narrates the mythical story, the second uses the character of Cassandra to prophesy future history, and the third section imagines the transcendence of history by the ideal hero who has endured all that tragedy can inflict. Thus the poem uses ancient story to illuminate, through perspective, all the tragedy of human history.

The theme of the poem can be described as the historic human struggle for power. Clytemnestra and her daughter Electra embody the ideal of mastery over man. But Cassandra assumes a new importance; she embodies that abstract knowledge which understands this historic struggle but cannot profit by it. Finally, Orestes achieves freedom from history through the renunciation both of power and the knowledge of it and through the mystical acceptance of the natural world. In terms of time Clytemnestra and Electra stand for power in the present, Cassandra for prophecy of time future, and Orestes for timelessness. But, of course, the poem succeeds, not because of its abstract form or ideas, but through the realization of these in poetic language and dramatic action.

The entire action of "The Tower Beyond Tragedy" takes place in the central square of Mycenae. This unity of place binds together the different actions and times encompassed by the poem. The story begins in the square with the return of King Agamemnon from the Trojan wars, and the narration emphasizes the historic pageantry of the occasion:

> The Queen's men were a hundred in the
> street and a hundred
> Lining the ramp, eighty on the great flags of the porch:
> she raising her white arms the spear-butts
> Thundered on the stone, and the shields clashed;

Soon the king retires to his bath, and meets death offstage.

In the second scene the queen returns to tell her subjects in riddles of the "sacrifice" she has performed; but Cassandra, speaking first in her own voice and then in the voice of the dead king, reveals the truth and accuses the queen. Then Clytemnestra, in the most remarkable passage in the poem, admits the truth to the soldiers; but she defies them (until her lover Aegistheus can arrive) first by the force of her will, and then by shedding her garments one by one in a kind of mythical strip-tease resembling that of Salome. This scene—grotesque as it must seem in prose summary—achieves a kind of hypnotic power in poetic narration. For the queen conquers the wills of both her political subjects and the men of Mycenae through the naked power of her sex. Not sensational so much as symbolic, this imagined action by the mythical queen incarnates the very principle of power—naked both in the figurative and in the literal sense.

The second section, or act, of this dramatic poem is introduced and then dominated by the prophecy of Cassandra. In a long passage whose poetry reaches imaginative heights, Cassandra prophesies the rise and fall of the empires of the earth. Beginning "If anywhere in the world / Were a tower with foundations," she sees "the world cataractlike / Pour screaming. . . ." Then, as the author indicates the beginning of part "II" in the midst of the prophecy, Cassandra foresees the modern world, proclaiming:

> A mightier to be cursed and a higher for malediction
> When America has eaten Europe and takes tribute of Asia,
>   when the ends of the world grow aware of each other
> And are dogs in one kennel.

By prophetic identification of time past with time future, Cassandra suggests the identity of all the empires of history in their struggle for power, and makes the myth of Clytemnestra the prototype of all. Then, after Orestes has killed his mother, the dying Cassandra prophesies according to tradition:

> And you haunted forever, never to sleep dreamless
>   again, never to see blue cloth
> But the red runs over it; fugitive of dreams, madman
>   at length, the memory of a scream following you
>   houndlike,
> Inherit Mycenae?

But Orestes concludes the "New Oresteia" by refusing to "inherit Mycenae." Renouncing the historic struggle for power, he escapes the Furies who otherwise would have made him fugitive. But where the classical dramatist had freed Orestes from the Furies by means of a formal trial and by reason of the vote of Athene, Jeffers frees him by means of a mystical experience beyond reason, which identifies him with non-human nature. Foreshadowing this, Act III opens with a dialogue between "the great stones" of the square of Mycenae, to whom Orestes appeals: "O stones of the house: I entreat hardness." His entreaty is finally granted, and at the end he explains to Electra: "I have fallen in love outward. . . . it is I that am like stone walking."

The mystical victory of Orestes, "who had climbed the tower beyond time, consciously, and cast humanity, entered the earlier fountain," forms the climax of "The Tower Beyond Tragedy."

The mystical idea remains obscure, but Jeffers was to return to it in later poems and we shall consider its implications in the chapter on his philosophy. But before this mystical conclusion, "The Tower Beyond Tragedy" had succeeded in dramatizing with imagination and effectiveness the universal human struggle for power.

V The Women at Point Sur

Following the success of his first long poems, Jeffers published *The Women at Point Sur*, which was—by universal consent— unsuccessful. But although the new poem failed, its failure was major, and the reasons for it important.

The Women at Point Sur was the only poem by Jeffers long enough to warrant separate publication, without the usual "other poems." Running to 175 pages, it was carefully planned, and developed a dramatic idea to a logical conclusion. Moreover, it included some of the best poetry and some of the most challenging ideas of its author. It failed not only because of its grotesque exaggeration of its dramatic ideas but because of the dead end to which its logic led. At its conclusion its hero "Lay down in the mouth of the black pit." But long before this, the average reader has laid the book down, exhausted by its imaginary exploration of all the dead-end canyons of this symbolic country.

After the critical and popular failure of this poem, Jeffers began seeking the reasons for it. His best explanation was contained in a letter to James Rorty: "Just as Ibsen in The Wild Duck made a warning against his own idea in the hands of a fool, so Point Sur was meant to be a warning, but at the same time a reassertion." The poem was indeed a warning against "the Roan Stallion idea of 'Breaking out of humanity,' misinterpreted in the mind of a fool or a lunatic," but its reassertion involved such violent exaggeration that the poem became almost a self-parody. As Jeffers suggested, other authors have done the same thing, but Ibsen's *Wild Duck* stopped short of parody. The nearest parallel is rather Melville's *Pierre*. Both works followed major successes by their authors, but both exaggerated the earlier tragic ideas almost to the point of burlesque; piling Pelion on Ossa, they merely achieved incredibility.

The Women at Point Sur tells the story of a Christian minister who has lost faith and retires to the wild country of Point Sur to proclaim that God is dead and that all laws have been annulled. Denying his Messiah, he himself seeks to become the new messiah: instead of "breaking out of humanity," he seeks disciples and new power over humanity. This is the perversion of Jeffers' idea: the hero who believes himself "falling in love outward," actually falls in love inward; and he symbolizes this delusion by committing incest with his daughter "April." Meanwhile he encourages a multiplicity of perversions among his disciples—who, it must be admitted, never needed much encouragement in the first place. The second half of the poem degenerates into a particularly ugly witches' sabbath.

The first half of *The Women at Point Sur*, however, achieves moments of great power before the reassertion of Jeffers' idea degenerates into the "lunatic" perversion of it. The Reverend Dr. Barclay's demonic search for ultimate truth recalls Ahab's "strike through the mask."

> ". . . There is a power behind appearances,
> you will break through to it and touch it.
> . . . I shall not die blind. Jesus did:
> 'why hast thou forsaken me, my God?'
> I not his son take him by violence. This is that hybris
> in the tragedy, that brings destruction.
> Content. I will buy."

But as the poem progresses, this titanic, single-minded search for truth becomes the divided and ambivalent quest for power and even self-indulgence:

> . . . The cold core of his mind
> Smiled at the rest, his mind was split into three parts,
> the cold core
> Observing the others, the first in full faith clear-eyed
> in bitter earnestness riding the tides of prophecy,
> The third watching the woman tremble and turn pale.

Therefore, in Section XII, Jeffers stops to comment on the degeneration of his characters:

> Here were new idols again to praise him;
> I made them alive; but when they looked up at the
> face before they had seen it they were drunken
> and fell down.
> . . . I sometime

> Shall fashion images great enough to face him
> A moment and speak while they die. These here have
>   gone mad: but stammer the tragedy you crackled
>   vessels.

The fact that Jeffers introduced this clear-eyed admission of comparative failure into the middle of his poem suggests, I think, that when he began writing, his intentions had not been entirely clear. The Reverend Dr. Barclay was first conceived as a titanic figure; but, in the course of the poem's action, he "went mad." Symbolically, his mind split into three parts: the first part still sought absolute truth, but the second part sought power, and the third part mere self-gratification. The "new idols" became "crackled vessels," and the second half of the "tragedy" "stammered" to its conclusion. What had started as high drama degenerated into a study of abnormal psychology.

But this interpretation tells only half the truth: all Jeffers' poems combine elements of high tragedy with those of abnormal psychology. The divided mind of Dr. Barclay mirrors the divisions of Jeffers' own mind: later he himself would abandon the disinterested expression of truth in order to preach political neutrality to an America at war. Like his Dr. Barclay, Jeffers also sometimes shared the messianic delusion, and like him he sometimes shared the vulnerability of the sensualist. The earlier long poems had kept these elements in balance; but *The Women at Point Sur* described their disintegration.

In one sense, this disintegration is the true subject of the poem. "Roan Stallion" had proclaimed that "Humanity . . . is the coal to break into fire, the atom to be split." And the new poem describes the splitting of the atom of human consciousness. That this purpose was conscious, Jeffers emphasized in his Prelude (which was also printed separately). Underlying the surface plot, the deeper subject of the poem is the inner "strain," common both to "humanity" and to physical matter:

> Always the strain, the straining flesh
>   who feels what God feels
> Knows the straining flesh, the aching desires,
> The enormous water straining its bounds, the electric
> Strain in the clouds, the strain of the oil in the
>   oil-tanks
> At Monterey, aching to burn, the strain of the spinning

> Demons that make an atom, straining to fly asunder,
> Straining to rest at the center,
> The strain in the skull, blind strains, force and
>   counter-force,
> Nothing prevails. . . .

When the atomic unity of human consciousness suddenly "breaks into fire," tragedy results, and a lightning flash of illumination occurs: this was the case in "Roan Stallion." But in *The Women at Point Sur* the repetitious series of human "explosions" caused only disintegration, and the "tragedy" stammered to a dead end.

VI *"Cawdor"*

"Cawdor," which followed *The Women at Point Sur*, differed from it in almost every particular. In "Cawdor" Jeffers described sane characters and normal actions; in the earlier poem he had described characters partly insane and actions often perverted. In the new poem he told its story in simple and realistic style, without interpolated sermons or apostrophes. Its setting lay in the heart of "Jeffers' country," and was described with concrete detail. In a note to his publishers Jeffers remarked: "I think of Cawdor as making a third with Tamar and The Women at Point Sur; but as if in Tamar human affairs had been seen looking westward, against the ocean; in Point Sur looking upward, minimized to ridicule against the stars; and in Cawdor looking eastward against the earth, reclaiming a little dignity from that association."

Because of its earth-fast realism and its "normal" human actions, "Cawdor" seemed to Jeffers' first biographer to be "his finest single volume." Except for one incident, the poem escaped from the realm of myth to that of contemporary reality, and pointed the way for the two later narrative poems whose localized characters and actions became even more fully naturalized in western life. But in seeking to abandon the mythical and the ideal, "Cawdor" cut itself off from the most characteristic and nourishing sources of Jeffers' poetic imagination. One incident in its plot remained so obviously mythical that it marred the dominant effect of pure realism.

"Cawdor" tells of an elderly widower who marries a young wife. The frustrated wife tries to seduce his son, and fails; then, like Potiphar's wife, she accuses the son. Tormented by jealousy, Cawdor kills the innocent young man. Finally, after learning the truth, he is driven by remorse to punish himself, like Oedipus, by gouging out his own eyes. Except for this final incident the plot is wholly modern, and the characters do "reclaim a little dignity" from their association with the earth. But it is hard to imagine a California rancher consciously gouging out his own eyes; the shadow of Oedipus mars the realistic effect. "Cawdor" remains a transitional narrative, midway between the earlier myths and the later tales.

It is significant that the most memorable passages in this realistic poem recall the poetic idealism and symbolism of the earlier myths. In his later volume of *Selected Poetry*, Jeffers excerpted from "Cawdor" an imaginative description of the "dream" of a dead man's brain just after death, and a second even more striking projection of the death-dream of a caged eagle. While in the realm of symbolism, "Fera" Martial, the untamed heroine, twice fits the skin of a recently killed mountain lion over her shoulders. She also identifies herself with the caged eagle, who has been shot through the wing, as she herself has been through the arm. The Shakespearean title seems meaningless, but "Cawdor's" attempt to explore the realm of contemporary reality borrows from Jeffers' earlier explorations of the realm of myth.

VII *"Dear Judas"*

Jeffers returned to traditional myth with "Dear Judas." This dramatic poem, which retells the familiar gospel story in unfamiliar terms, is remarkable in every way. Its challenging interpretation of the personality of Jesus has inevitably alienated many orthodox readers. But the psychological reasonableness of the interpretation, which emphasizes biblical incidents often glossed over, and the deeply felt veneration of the poet for his protagonist, despite an apparent impiety, combines with a genuine poetic exaltation to create a memorable work of art. The heresy of its interpretation will probably prevent wide acceptance of the poem. But for originality of thought, artistry of conception, and beauty of expression, the poem ranks high; its controversial excellence has been recognized by dramatists and theologians, as well as by poets and critics.

The form of "Dear Judas" emphasizes its mythical quality. Jeffers specifically "chose the method of the Japanese Nō plays, which present a haunted place and passion's afterglow, two or three ghosts or echoes of life, re-enacting in a dream their ancient deeds and sorrows."[2] The characters slowly materialize out of a remembrance of time past, seek to recall the motivations of their former deeds, and re-enact them in a mood of retrospective abstraction. Realism is deliberately abandoned in order to emphasize, on the one hand, the mythical distance, and on the other, the search for abstract truth. This unrealism would diminish any other story, but the gospel narrative remains so emotionally charged that a mere "passion's afterglow" still arouses intense contemporary emotion.

The psychological interpretations of Jesus' personality have particularly antagonized the orthodox. First, this Jesus is described as claiming to be the son of God because he refuses to accept the truth of his own illegitimacy. Second, he is described as seeking power over men's minds in future time by means of his consciously sought martyrdom:

> . . . Oh, power
> Bought at the price these hands and feet and all this body
>   perishing in torture will pay is holy
> Their minds love terror, their souls cry to be sacrificed
>   for. . . .
>   I go a stranger passage to a greater dominion,
> More tyrannous, more terrible, more true, than Caesar or
>   any subduer of earth before him has dared to dream
>   of . . .

This new interpretation of "the only divine figure still living in the minds of people of our race" denies Jesus' divinity on two counts: physically, he is not the son of God; spiritually, he does not seek to transcend history, but to dominate it. He is a demigod, or titan, whose "belief / Has lifted you up to over-dream nature." These negations of Christian doctrine were bound to alienate readers. Jeffers himself omitted the poem from his *Selected Poetry*; and later, when the drama was staged in 1947, it was banned both in Boston and in Maine.

However, this new interpretation of the character of Jesus is based upon facts recorded in the gospels. Jeffers has pointed out that:

> The mind of Jesus is . . . very far from simple. . . . It is deep, powerful and beautiful; and strangely complex; not wholly integrated. He is the Prince of Peace, yet He came "not to bring peace but a sword." He is gentle and loving, yet He drives men with whips from the temple. He calls down destruction on Jerusalem, His curse kills an innocent fig tree.
>
> This is not the mind of a mere incarnation of love, as the sentimentalists represent him, but of a man of genius, a poet and a leader.[2]

Driving the money-lenders from the Temple and cursing Jerusalem and the fig tree, this new Jesus seems very human—and also very believable.

In spite of this new conception of Jesus as "not wholly integrated"—partly indeed because of it—Jeffers' new mythical protagonist captures both our imagination and our sympathy. He still preserves the traditional attributes: he loves mankind, and he particularly loves the one disciple who betrays him. Jeffers has emphasized this: "My title is deceptive, perhaps. The emphasis should be on the word 'dear'—'dear' Judas—the man was dear to Jesus even while he was being betrayed by him."[2] But loving humanity, Christ prefers greatness to the peace which Judas desires. Jesus seeks to show men the way to power through suffering:

> Only a crucified
> God can fill the wolf bowels of Rome, only a torture high
> up in the air, and crossed beams, hang sovereign
> When the blond savages exalt their kings; when the north
> moves, and the hairy-breasted north is unbound,
> And Caesar a mouse under the hooves of the horses.

In opposition to Judas, who would "get the firebrand locked up, . . . save the city," this new Jesus preaches rebellion against Caesar, albeit a largely non-violent rebellion of the mind.

In *Theology and Modern Literature*, Amos Wilder (brother of Thornton) has analyzed "Dear Judas" at some length and considered the poem as typical of a modern attitude toward Christianity. Its "emphasis on suffering as the clue to the appeal of Christ and Christianity" has appeared frequently in modern literature, including Yeats and D. H. Lawrence. But Dr. Wilder points out that Jeffers goes beyond these to affirm the transcendent greatness of Jesus: Jeffers "only rejects and denies in order to carry out his role of celebrant the more effectively. . . . His affirmation is in terms of a cosmic mysticism which must be distinguished from all usual forms of pantheism." And beyond "Dear Judas," Dr. Wilder points out that "the best [of Jeffers' poems] take on the character, at least in their climaxes, of hymns to salvation."

The excellence of "Dear Judas" consists partly in the originality of its conception, partly in the power of its language. Jesus explains his purpose and justifies it against the charge of cruelty:

> But what are men *now?*
> Are the bodies free, or the minds full of clear light,
> or the hearts fearless? I having no foothold but slippery
> Broken hearts and despairs, the world is so heaped
> against me, am yet lifting my peoples nearer
> In emotion, and even at length in powers and perception,
> to the universal God than ever humanity
> Has climbed before.

The single, daring image, or metaphor of "no foothold but slippery / Broken hearts and despairs" makes visual the whole emotional struggle of Christianity; and the development of this image by means of the verbs "lifting" and "climbing" also develops the idea and emphasizes the truth of the theologian's description of the poem as a "hymn to salvation."

Yet a serious doubt remains: Jeffers' Jesus is the hero of a tragedy, but Jeffers' ideal hero who achieves perfect salvation must go "beyond tragedy." In "The Tower Beyond Tragedy" Orestes achieved this ultimate salvation by renouncing power. But Jesus is driven by the desire for power, and therefore fails to transcend tragedy, or history. Indeed, he is described as lusting for power and as seeking a dominion "more tyrannous" than Caesar's. The one character in "Dear Judas" who has achieved true salvation, according to Jeffers, is Lazarus; and Lazarus is described not so much as resurrected from death but as speaking with the accent of death. He has "an unchangeable bluish face," and is addressed by Judas as "Bluebottle." Part of the shock which "Dear Judas" usually causes is due not so much to its unorthodoxy as to its criticism of Jesus' "lust" for power and to its praise of Lazarus' deathlike negation of life.

Yet Jeffers praised Jesus, and all the other heroic figures of tragedy, because of this very lust for life. And he specifically celebrated Jesus, through the mouth of Lazarus, because of his domination of history. Lazarus addresses Mary:

> Your son has chosen what men are not able to do;
> He has chosen and made his own fate. The Roman Caesar
> will call your son his master and his God; the floods
> That wash away Caesar and divide the booty, shall worship
> your son. The unconjectured selvages
> And closed orbits of the ocean ends of the earth shall
> hear of him.

And later, comparing "Dear Judas" with the companion poem "The Loving Shepherdess," Jeffers implicitly praised Jesus for the "efficiency" of his love: "There is some relationship of thought between the two longer poems in this book; the shepherdess in the one, and Judas and Jesus in the other, each embodying different aspects of love: nearly pure, therefore undefiled but quite inefficient in the first; pitying in the second; possessive in the third." Thus Jeffers celebrated Jesus as the greatest tragic figure in human history; but, because he imagined an ideal beyond tragedy, he also criticized Jesus for his lust for life and his desire for spiritual power.

VIII *"The Loving Shepherdess"*

By contrast, "The Loving Shepherdess" imagined a tragic heroine whose love is selfless and who is in many ways the opposite of Jesus: Clare Walker embodies the eternal feminine in its purest form, without any admixture of the masculine desire for power. Her tragic story is unique in Jeffers' poetry, and perhaps in literature: her character was suggested by a character in Sir Walter Scott, but her story is told without romantic sentiment. "The torches of violence" which lighted the crucifixion of Jesus have burned down, and the pure flame of non-possessive love glows steadily. This poem, alone among Jeffers' narratives, illustrates his occasional ability to describe "humanity" with simplicity and dignity.

But after writing the poem, Jeffers described its story somewhat cynically: "The Gentle Shepherdess is the story of one who has committed self-sacrifice . . . a saint, I suppose, going up to a natural martyrdom, aureoled with such embellishments as the mind of time permits. Incapable of taking thought for herself, she wanders the length of the coast that has usually been the scene of my verses." But Clare Walker "has committed self-sacrifice" for a motive far different from that of Jesus: although a doctor has warned her that conceiving another child will cost her life, she will not deny nature, and "incapable of taking thought for herself," follows her fate to its tragic end. Her love, neither possessive nor sensuous, is "nearly pure" in its selfless love of all mankind: it is as if Jeffers had—almost by accident— created a "saint" whose "human" nature is also perfectly natural, but after having created this human perfection, accused his heroine of "committing self-sacrifice."

"The Loving Shepherdess" is the most completely "natural" of all Jeffers' long poems; it is almost free from doctrine or diatribe. Its form is the natural form of "the long journey," which is also man's long journey toward death. And the human characters are the scattered ranchers and laborers of "Jeffers' country," some of whom we have met in the earlier poems. But more important than these human characters are the individual-ized sheep of Clare Walker's flock, who one by one disappear or die during the course of the journey, and who symbolize the illusions of security and happiness which disappear in the course of man's life. At the end, one of Jeffers' most effective passages foreshadows the heroine's fate, linking the human world with the natural by analogy:

> Far up the Carmel Valley
> The river became a brook, she watched a salmon
> Row its worn body up-stream over the stones
> And struck by a thwart current expose the bruised
> White belly to the white of the sky, gashed with red wounds,
>   but right itself
> And wriggle up-stream, having that within it, spirit or
>   desire,
> Will spend all its dear flesh and all the power it has
>   gathered, in the sweet salt pastures and fostering
>   ocean,
> To find the appointed high-place and perish.

Unlike Jesus and Judas, whose martyrdom and suicide are the results of human cruelty and betrayal, Clare Walker's tragedy seems to share the inevitability of nature.

IX *"Thurso's Landing"*

After writing "Dear Judas," Jeffers spent a year in Great Britain and Ireland, after which he published a volume of short poems, *Descent to the Dead*. "Thurso's Landing" appeared three long years after "Dear Judas," and marks the beginning of a new period. "Thurso" contrasts with "Dear Judas" in every way: it is contemporary, realistic, and almost completely non-mythical. Jeffers himself so described it: "It is about as long as Cawdor and seems to me the best thing I have yet written. The scene is a canyon of the coast south of Monterey, widened by an episode into the Arizona desert. The time is perhaps more distinctly near the present than usual in my verses; the persons seem to me a little more conscious of the moral implications of what they do." If present-day reality, local scenery, and self-conscious morality constitute excellence, Jeffers' estimate of his new poem was correct, and many of his critics have praised "Thurso" for these virtues. But this poem inevitably renounced the major virtues of his earlier myths: the multiple meanings of traditional action patterns, the archetypal appeal of timeless character types, and—most important—the deeply felt compulsion of motivations springing from the subconscious mind. After "Dear Judas" Jeffers wrote no more pure myths, and—in my opinion, at least—his narrative poetry suffered as a result.

The action and mood of "Thurso's Landing" are of an unrelieved bleakness. The theme of the poem, as Jeffers has pointed out, is "courage"; but courage is a negative virtue, and some warmth of passion is needed to make it—and the characters who act it out—acceptable. Only the young wife, Helen Thurso, supplies this warmth, and soon it is extinguished when her husband Reave pursues her and her runaway lover to the desert and, by sheer force of will, compels her to return to his barren ranch. After this the problem becomes one of endurance: Reave Thurso is crippled while attempting to dismantle his father's obsolete cable machinery, but his contempt for his father's earlier suicide now fortifies his blind determination to live on. After one unsuccessful attempt to end his crippling agony, Helen Thurso finally kills him and then poisons herself. The tragedy is wholly unrelieved, and not wholly credible.

The comparative failure of "Thurso's Landing" is caused partly by the poet's ambivalence about "morality." The hero clearly re-

calls Milton's *Samson Agonistes,* and the heroine his Dalilah.
Twice the language echoes Milton. Helen Thurso early berates
her husband:

> ". . . you've never let yourself go,
> . . . there's no nature in you, nothing but . . . noble . . .
> Nothing but . . . one of those predestined stone men
> For women to respect and cheat."

But later she accepts his rigid morality:

> "Nothing can break you,
> It was only bones and nerves broke, nothing can change you,
> Now I've begun to know good from bad
> I can be straight too."

And at the end Reave Thurso reasserts: "There's nothing good
in it / Except the courage in us not to be beaten." In "Thurso's
Landing" Milton's "courage never to submit or yield" has become
petrified in a "stone man," and the self-conscious moral heroism
of the characters seems almost to diminish the poem. The
"cataract life" of "Tamar," and the "torchlike" magnificence of
"Dear Judas" have frozen into a modern morality. When at the
end the poet reasserts that

> . . . It is rather ignoble in its quiet times,
>   mean in its pleasures,
> Slavish in the mass; but at stricken moments it can
>   shine terribly against the dark magnificence of things.

the language of the poetry is noble, but we feel that the story
has failed fully to illuminate the "dark magnificence" which the
poet affirms.

X *"Give Your Heart to the Hawks"*

"Give Your Heart to the Hawks" is the most successful of
these purely realistic narrative poems dealing with the California
coast and its people. Jeffers wrote to his publishers that "in
poetry and dramatic value, and variety of character, it seems to
me rather better perhaps than Thurso. . . . The scene is contemporary." In contrast to its predecessor, the action and mood
are skilfully modulated, the interplay of character creates interesting situations, and even the changes of scenery relieve the

oppressively monolithic mood of the earlier poem. This is the most "modern" of all the long poems, and—except perhaps for its final scenes—the most natural and convincing.

Most important, "Give Your Heart to the Hawks" develops a major idea through a series of dramatic actions to a logical conclusion; and this idea is of a piece with the scene, the time, and the characters. In the deepest sense, this poem is a "Western," centering upon the historic conflict between those who take the law (and the punishment) into their own hands, and those who follow the moral regulations of society. To a certain extent, therefore, this poem is also a "morality" but the issues are not predetermined, the treatment is not conventional, the morality is not arbitrary, and the judgment is not self-conscious.

The first major scene describes a beach party at the foot of the cliffs with a powerful realism. Approaching the ocean:

> . . . on the airy brink
> Above the great slides of the thousand foot cliff.
> They were very gay, colorful mites on the edge of
> the world.

But on the beach the human "mites" get drunk, quarrel, and separate. Then Lance Fraser comes upon his brother Michael making love to Lance's wife Fayne; in drunken anger he kills him. The killing has not been seen by the others, and Fayne urges that, since it was wholly impulsive and natural, it should not be confessed but reported as an accident:

> "When Arriba and his boys
> Stole cows of ours, did you run to the courthouse?
> We take care of ourselves down here. What we have done
> Has to be borne. It's in ourselves and there's no escaping,
> The state of California can't help you bear it.
> That's only a herd of people, the state.
> Oh, give your heart to the hawks for a snack of meat
> But not to men."

However, her husband is the son of a religious moralist, and cannot believe in her doctrine of self-punishment, although he agrees to try.

The second half of the poem describes the struggle of wills, or moralities, between husband and wife. Both are wholly western:

> . . . He was like this mountain coast,
> All beautiful, with chances of brutal violence; precipitous,
>   dark-natured, beautiful; without humor, without ever
> A glimmer of gaiety; blind gray headland and arid mountain,
>   and trailing from his shoulders the infinite ocean.

But this time the wife is dominant, and the two leave the father's ranch to wander down the coast seeking freedom from the world and their own past. Lance, however, cannot free himself from guilt; he compulsively punishes himself by dragging his hands across barbed wire and has recurring nightmares recalling his crime. He goes mad, and imagining a herd of cows to be his tormentors, he blindly attacks them. Finally, realizing his own madness, he throws himself off the cliff to the rocks below.

These final scenes of self-punishment and madness seem unrealistic, and suggest something of the mythical madness of Don Quixote, who also attacked a herd of cows: to this extent the final scenes detract from the realism of the poem. But the progressive deterioration of the hero inevitably follows from the nature of his character and belief, whereas the self-reliance of his wife, Fayne, is equally convincing. Before the end she exhorts him: "We have come out of the world and are free." But she finally realizes that "I could never help you at all, / And now has come the wild end." But still she assures herself: "I could not keep you, but your child in my body / Will change the world." Is this assertion of faith in the future mere self-delusion? Or is it prophetic? The poem refuses to judge: only in terms of the earlier action can any moral be projected.

XI   *"Solstice" and "At the Birth of an Age"*

Solstice and Other Poems marked a sudden and ominous break in the progression of Jeffers' narrative poetry. The title poem, which continued the realistic narratives dealing with the California coast, failed completely; and at the other extreme, "At the Birth of an Age" explored the vein of philosophical myth which had been opened with "The Tower Beyond Tragedy" and "Dear Judas," but divided sharply between mythical narrative and poetic philosophy. Radcliffe Squires has described this split between realistic action and idealistic reflection as characteristic of all Jeffers' poetry, and has praised "The Double Axe" for its perfect formal expression of it.

After "Give Your Heart to the Hawks," it is true, Jeffers wrote no narratives successfully integrating realism with myth. But his best earlier poems had successfully accomplished this integration. And the later division symbolized by "The Double Axe" was to prove artistically dangerous. After 1935 his realistic narratives of modern life tended toward an unrelieved ugliness, and his commentaries on contemporary history sometimes amounted to mere name-calling. Meanwhile his later mythical narratives often lost sight of the human actions and passions whose archetypes they were, and consequently suffered from abstraction. With "Solstice" the nature of his narrative poetry changed.

Although "Solstice" gave its name to the new volume, it was printed after "At the Birth of an Age" and was far inferior to that poem. By general consent, "Solstice" is Jeffers' worst narrative poem; but it is so very bad that it is interesting. "Solstice" may fairly be described as a caricature of a poem: both the narrative action and the poetic diction approach the grotesque. The line between the sublime and the ridiculous is proverbially thin; and, although Jeffers' best poetry achieves magnificence, this poem becomes ridiculous. One metaphor will illustrate: "The gas-line dripped stinking blood, and the car died." But more spectacular (because more recognizably Jeffersian) is the melodramatic description of a symbolic sunset:

> . . . A fountain of intense light
> Poured on the ocean and sprayed and scattered; but now
>   too late for gold, redder than blood, great waves
> Of blood-color light, that stained the sea they came from
>   and treacherously
> From below stabbed the cloud, dyeing its unguarded belly
>   with fiery blood, and beat the sea-wall
> Mountain so that it rang like a gong
> Resounding with sanguine light.

This overwrought narrative of a Californian Medea rings as loud—and as hollow—as a gong.

In writing "At the Birth of an Age" Jeffers consciously turned his back on realism and adopted the form of philosophic myth, interpreted poetically. Like "Dear Judas" the poem begins with a frank statement emphasizing the historical remoteness of the action, and continues to sketch chapters of the Niblung Saga by means of brief dramatic scenes. The central figures of Gudrun and her brothers—betraying and betrayed—act out their parts against a background of recurrent battles and alarums. Then, after her brothers have all been killed, Gudrun realizes her own confused treachery and commits suicide.

But the mythical action suggested by the Niblung Saga is only introductory to the central concern of this poem—the description of the historic transition from the pagan materialism of the late Roman age to the new religion of the Middle Ages that Jeffers represents as a mixture of Christianity, Promethean mythology, and the Norse worship of "the hanged god." Before the death of Gudrun, one realistic scene, played against the background of a painting of the god Prometheus chained to Mount Elboros, confronts Attila with a Christian bishop who argues the Christian doctrine of submission and mercy. But with the death of Gudrun, the background painting of the hanged god becomes the foreground of the poem, and it is materialized by the imagination of "Gudrun's Shadow," which stands aloof invoking this new god and observing his worship. The poetic language, which suggests the confusion between reality and dream in Gudrun's soul, is often hauntingly beautiful.

The final scenes of "At the Birth of an Age" describe in generalized language the Promethean-Christian religion of "the hanged god;" they consist of speeches by the god, interspersed with pleas by his worshipers, and with detached observations by "Gudrun's Shadow." This religious philosophy is both interesting and original (the next chapter will consider it in more detail), and the poetic diction is often effective; but its relation to the earlier action is tenuous, and its abstraction difficult. The philosophy and the poetic language challenge comparison with "Dear Judas," and they sometimes clarify and enlarge the interpretations of that poem; but the vital connection between living character and action, and the resulting religious psychology and interpretation, has partly been lost. The disunity of the poem is clearly purposeful, and its form suggests that of "The Double Axe"; but "At the Birth of an Age" appeals more to the mind than to the emotions.

XII *"Such Counsels"*

"Such Counsels You Gave to Me" develops the realistic mode of "Solstice" rather than the mythical philosophy of "At the Birth of an Age." But where "Solstice" had narrated its tale of confused violence in overwrought language, the new poem tells its similar tale in almost prosaic dialogue and description. The story concerns a medical student who, suffering a nervous breakdown, is invalided home. Fully conscious of his own mental illness, he nevertheless blames it on his mother's adultery and his father's penury; in his hatred he poisons the father. The narration shares something of the confusion of its subject, but it conveys a vivid impression of a divided mind at war with itself. Lacking any resolution of its moral anarchy, however, the poem ends negatively: "there are certain duties / Even for . . . what did you say? . . . modern man." Although conscious of his own delusion, this neurotic hero is described as the norm of the modern man.

A contrast of "Such Counsels" with "Margrave," Jeffers' earlier and shorter poem about a neurotic medical student, is illuminating. In "Margrave" the author had viewed his subject objectively; using the young man's neurotic delusion to illustrate the sickness of modern civilization but contrasting it clearly with the norm of sanity in nature. In "Such Counsels," however, the author has identified the point of view with his young protagonist, so that the neurotic confusion is internalized; the norm by which it might have been measured and judged has disappeared.

Jeffers seems now to be saying: "such counsels" as these lead to insanity, but insanity is the norm of the modern world, therefore it must be accepted as normal. Although his poetry has never been hopeful, these counsels are not of despair but of confusion. The timeless ideal of sanity in nature gave a sense of proportion to his early poetry; and although he described this ideal as practically unattainable, the tension between the impossible ideal and the intolerable actual contributed to his great power. Now his realistic poetry has omitted the ideal. "Such Counsels" seems written from within the nightmare, without any perspective of conscious sanity. It suggests a clinical case history offered without comment by an unhappy analyst.

This loss of normal perspective, which diminishes all the realistic narrative poems of this period, is partly the result of the poet's "obsession with contemporary history," which he acknowledges but laments in his prefatory note to his next volume, *Be Angry at the Sun*. In "Such Counsels" the promiscuous sister of the young hero was named "France," and the characters compare their own confusions with those of the world about them. *Be Angry at the Sun* includes a "masque" about Hitler, entitled

"The Bowl of Blood." And "Mara," the chief poem of this new volume, describes how

> . . . . a passionate voice
> Barking a foreign language beat through the room
> under the sounding-box
> Of the steep roof, bringing no meaning but emotion,
> Scorn and dog wrath, cored on the wailing of a lost child,
> To this far shore. Old Ferguson snapped it silent
> And said, "What's that?" She said, "Hitler, I guess.
> They're starting a war."

The brief title poem which concludes the volume admonishes sagely: "Be angry at the sun / If these things anger you." But the longer narrative poems imply the poet's personal anger at the setting of the sun on his own "perishing republic."

The first section of "Mara" states its theme explicitly:

> . . . he lived the best
> Of possible lives for a man of his race, a cattle-driving
> And horseback life on his own place, on the free mountains;
> And intelligent enough to know it the best;
> And married to a beautiful girl, all wants fulfilled:
> not his own life chiefly
> But life in general looked dirty, senseless and destitute
> In his dark times.

But as the poem develops, the "best" life of this hero not only "looks" but progressively becomes "dirty"; at the end young Ferguson, unable to endure it, commits suicide. Apparently his life has been corrupted by the modern world, and, within the formal limits of the narrative poem, this world sees itself damned once again. But in a later, brief poem, Jeffers gives his true, personal criticism of this "best" hero:

> Tomorrow I will take up that heavy poem again
> About Ferguson, deceived and jealous man
> Who bawled for the truth, the truth, and failed to endure
> Its first least gleam.

In other words this narrative, which explicitly describes the life of a modern hero, denies this hero either honesty or courage. And then—worst of all—it does not permit the reader to recognize that the author really considers his hero less then ideal. Like

"Such Counsels," "Mara" describes a modern nightmare without providing any conscious perspective or illumination on it. It is as if the author, while composing his narrative poem, had shared in the nightmare, and had regained his conscious sanity only after dreaming the poem.

XIII The Double Axe

The Double Axe, published seven years later, marked a striking change in Jeffers' narrative technique. The first long poem, "The Love and the Hate," described events frankly supernatural. And the second, "The Inhumanist," developed the poetry of mythical interpretation first exemplified in "At the Birth of an Age" and combined realistic narrative with a kind of supernatural counterpoint of poetic myth.

"The Love and the Hate" developed the same nightmare emotions earlier described realistically in "Such Counsels" and "Mara," but these are now described in terms of a frank supernaturalism. Yet the word "realistic" is misleading: both the earlier poems had introduced ghostly "alter egos" or "shadow" counterparts of their protagonists, but only to suggest their delusions. Now "The Love and the Hate" describes the actual return of a young soldier, who had been killed in the Pacific war, to his California home. Supernaturally, this soldier has willed his body to rise from the grave and return to confront his fanatically patriotic father with the facts of suffering and death. The action is still narrated "realistically," but what had been the deluded imagination of the hero has now become a supernatural fact. What had been events which *seemed* like nightmare has now *become* a nightmare seeming like actual events. The nightmare has been externalized.

"The Love and the Hate" is an extremely unpleasant narrative poem. In "Dear Judas," Lazarus had returned from the grave, with a bluish face and dressed in earth-stained cerements, in order to speak with the living. But now Hoult Gore returns from the dead, with putrescent flesh and the odor of decomposition, in order actively to destroy his living enemies. One of Edgar Allen Poe's tales of the grotesque describes a dead man willing himself to live for several days after death until he accomplishes a purpose, at which point his body decomposes all at once. Now Jeffers describes a physically decomposing body as both speaking, acting, and—simultaneously—stinking. In discussing "Classic American Literature" D. H. Lawrence had emphasized its pre-dcliction for "post mortem effects." Now post mortem actions, described realistically, produce mortal effects. The nightmare has not only been externalized, but has realized itself in the active imagination. The horrors of the Grand Guignol pale in comparison.

Considered by itself, "The Love and the Hate" is simply nightmarish. But the title is a misnomer, for the poem omits "the love" and describes only "the hate"—and that in a form so extreme that only the all-consuming holocaust with which it ends can exorcise its nightmare of evil. Where "Tamar" had ended with the burning of "the house," this poem ends with the burning of the whole country in a forest fire. And these hate-fed flames suggest the inferno of all modern civilization:

> "Oh, oh, look down there, that's hell
> And we are in it. The boiler of life and death: you can
> see faces: there's Tojo, there's Roosevelt."

But this long poem of hate is only the first of the two which constitute *The Double Axe*. The holocaust is intended to burn off the evil of modern civilization, clearing the ground for the second poem. "The Inhumanist" begins:

> An old man with a double-bit axe
> Is caretaker at the Gore place. The cattle, except
> a few wild horns, died in that fire.

But "the caretaker at the Gore place," who is the hero of "The Inhumanist," is no ordinary mortal. He is a mythical hero; and, in some ways, he is most interesting of all the creations of his author. In this poem Jeffers for the first time has imagined a purely original religious myth; for "Dear Judas" had been historical, and all his other original myths had been secular. "The Inhumanist" is closely related to the biblical Book of Job, yet both its conception and its dramatization are completely unconventional, and—for instance—utterly unlike Archibald Mac-Leish's realistic dramatization of "J. B." "The caretaker at the Gore place" hears the voice of God speaking from the storm-wind; he argues with various visitors, both human and supernatural, who trespass upon his domain; he meets and destroys "the man of sorrows," an alter ego who would reinvolve him with the world; and finally he becomes "care-free" and able to welcome with equanimity a series of "panting fugitives" fleeing "the end of the world." In one sense all of Jeffers' best narrative poems have been "hymns to salvation," as Amos Wilder has called them. But only "The Inhumanist" is, by conscious intention, a religious drama of salvation.

"The Inhumanist," however, is not simply a religious drama; it is a very complex poem. Its techniques are partly realistic, partly supernatural, partly symbolic, and partly philosophic. The old man is at once a caretaker, a hermit, an observer of human folly, and a seeker after divine truth. The double axe which he carries is at once a practical tool, a symbol of generation, an instrument of divine destruction, and a source of inhuman wisdom ("you have killed the lies men live by"). The poem exists on many levels.

Realistically, "The Inhumanist" continues the theme of "the love and the hate" developed in the earlier poem. The old caretaker is soon joined by a daughter, of whose existence he had been ignorant, but whom he welcomes out of natural necessity. The daughter is soon involved with the owner of a neighboring ranch; she suffers violence at the hands of his hate-driven wife and her kinfolk; and eventually she runs away with her lover. Meanwhile the hate-full neighbors inflict and suffer further violence upon each other, until the gibbering ghost of the last one begs, and receives, final release from the double axe in the hands of the old man. The combination of realistic and supernatural violence which constituted the whole plot of the earlier poem, now constitutes the human background of the new poem against which the old man both acts out, and thinks out, his inhumanistic drama.

Simultaneously with the realistic narrative, and in alternating sections, the old man and his mysterious double axe act out a symbolic drama which ends with his final disinvolvement from the human tragedy. First a dog adopts him, then the daughter claims his protection, and from time to time a series of trespassers intrude upon his solitude to importune or to debate with him. One man wishes to make the Gore place public, another wishes to become his disciple, a crowd comes seeking to found the socialist state, a pure scientist seeks escape from governmental compulsion, and groups of other refugees from civilization appear on various errands. Meanwhile the old man's alter ego intrudes with two mysterious thieves to "betray" him. But after an intense inner struggle the old man with the double axe kills the other half of himself, saying:

> "No man has ever known himself or surpassed himself
>   until he has killed
> Half of himself."

Freed of this "self-murdered half-self," he ends his days in superhuman equanimity.

Simultaneously with this drama of symbolic action, both the framework and the pattern of the poem consist of a series of self-questions and dialogues between the old man and his second self, and with his God. Explicitly the poem begins with three bare questions: "Does God exist?" "Not an anthropoid God?" and "A conscious God?" As the various actions develop, they suggest various answers: "I see he despises happiness," and "he wants what man's feeling for beauty wants," and "man is no measure of anything." Then in the wilderness:

> While he [the Inhumanist] considered the matter, staring upward,
>   and the night's noises
> Hushed, there came down from heaven a great virile cry,
>   a voice hoarser than thunder heavily reverberated
> Among the star-whorls and cliffs of darkness: "I am caught.
>   I am in the net."

Realistically, the old man believes this voice that is perhaps the reflex of his own imagination, but the "great virile cry" is both real and imagined. Later, when the pure scientist debates with him, the Inhumanist both defends and defines his own worship of God against the materialism of the scientist; the old man praises "A contemplation of God" and "A coming nearer to God, . . . to learn his ways / And love his beauty." Both by intention and by result, the poem is deeply religious.

"The Inhumanist" is certainly the most interesting and probably the best of all Jeffers' later poems. But the question of its ultimate success and excellence is still doubtful. The many disparate elements which constitute the poem do not always cohere. The bare intellectual framework does not seem to fit the realistic action which it encloses. Moreover, this action repeats the emotional insanities which have characterized all the later narratives; and we remember the poet's earlier warning to himself in "Margrave":

> . . . to speak of . . . the abject
> Horror, would be to insult humanity more than it deserves.

The realistic extremes of *The Double Axe* insult humanity too much; only the superhuman detachment which "The Inhumanist" finally achieves can balance the earlier excesses.

XIV *"Hungerfield"*

Jeffers' last long poem, "Hungerfield," achieves a kind of resolution of these conflicts, and it is a fitting finale to this series of myths exploring the fate of modern man. Short as it is, "Hungerfield" achieves a strange fusion of the supernatural, the natural, and the personal. Where "Roan Stallion" had retold ancient myth in natural terms, "Hungerfield" now imagines a supernatural myth for the modern world: the two poems are equally brief, but, in their different styles, equally effective.

This "rough hero Hungerfield" becomes a modern counterpart of the mythical Hercules; but, curiously, his actions now change and supernaturalize the Greek story. The last labor of Hercules was to drag Cerberus up from Hades; and Homer earlier mentioned a forgotten myth about Hercules wounding the god Hades himself. Now Hungerfield literally wrestles with the angel of death for the life of his dying mother, Alcmena Hungerfield, and for a time destroys the natural order of things. But the violence of his action, as well as the emotional violence which has motivated it, destroys both his family and his house; finally only the old mother is left, hopelessly praying for death. This last poem is fully as grim as the others.

Now, however, the emotional violence has been rendered acceptable. The dying mother, who has been forced to live in pain beyond her time, curses the son and imagines hateful lies for him about his brother and his young wife. These two soon feel his inner anger, and the wife, "Arab," flees in despair to drown herself in the ocean. But this localized myth suddenly enlarges to become a metaphor of all the modern world:

> "I think you're still troubled by the drug,
> Mother," he answered; and Arab's child

> Began to wail like a little dog that has lost its master.
>   He is all alone by the bombed house,
> And they never come home; he sits in the empty gate, his
>   mouth small and rounded, turned straight to heaven,
> Starving, and wails.

Hungerfield becomes the modern hero who by instinct fights off death, only to cause more death by the very violence of his hatred, this time unjustified. But unlike his mythical predecessors, he is truly heroic in his way, and his wife and brother are truly faithful to him. Only the blind human refusal to be reconciled to the fact of death has motivated the tragedy.

Meanwhile, this supernatural myth is framed by the poet's memory of his own wife's actual death and by his own final acceptance of and reconciliation with it. Unlike "The Inhumanist," which was framed by intellectual questions about God and metaphysical truth, this poem is motivated by feelings of personal immediacy. The mythical hero seems to become the poet's own alter ego, who had formerly recoiled from all the violence and death of the modern world, but whose symbolic destruction now reconciles the poet to it. The insanities of emotion which have characterized all the later poems recur once again, but the supernatural myth gives them distance, the poet's technical skill and psychological insight give them verisimilitude, and his personal experience and suffering give them immediacy and conviction.

CHAPTER 3

The Short Poems

IN THE COURSE of a long career Jeffers has published hundreds of poems, varying in length from 175 pages to eight lines, and of almost every conceivable length between. Yet the division of "The Long Poems" from "The Short Poems" is not so arbitrary as it seems. The longer poems are all narratives of a sort, and most of them deal with the materials of myth. The shorter poems rarely narrate actions; and when they do, the actions are used for purposes of fable or apologue. Instead of the imagined world of fiction and myth, the short poems usually deal with the familiar world of here and now. And instead of the irrational and ambivalent emotions of the subconscious, the short poems describe and interpret the more "normal" and rational aspects of experience.

Although the techniques of myth, which dominate Jeffers' long poems, were universal in primitive times and have continued to dominate the literature of many Oriental countries, they have proved less popular in the Western world and in the Age of Reason. Therefore, perhaps, many readers and critics have preferred Jeffers' short poems. These have seemed to enjoy a "freedom from excess" which has characterized the long narratives. They have preserved "a more even quality." And they have been judged "better works of art." Of course it may be argued that the art of the lyric only seems better (because more obvious) than the art of the novel, but the new critics have exalted the lyric over the novel, and modern taste has disliked the old-fashioned, narrative poem.

The short poems of Jeffers not only differ from the long ones, but possess virtues of their own. They are as unconventional as the long ones, and show an even greater variety. Very few are lyrics in the strict sense, although many give expression to a single emotion, and a few actually sing. Perhaps the phrase "meditative lyric" best describes the largest number. Some of the longer poems, such as "Apology for Bad Dreams," have been called "free odes." And "The Humanist's Tragedy" and "Margrave" are clearly fables, or apologues. But the majority defy strict classification, having a form, and often a subject matter, entirely their own.

Some of these short poems are primarily autobiographical and have been discussed in the chapter on the poet's life. But unlike the long narratives, these short poems do not illustrate any clear evolution of style or attitude, and therefore do not lend themselves to strict chronological treatment. Many, which are purely philosophical, will be considered in the next chapter. In this chapter we may analyze a few typical poems in some detail, and suggest the "singularity" which distinguishes them, just as the techniques of myth have distinguished the longer poems.

All Jeffers' short poems involve the description and the interpretation of experience. This interpretation, sometimes implicit, is suggested by means of perspective, or symbol, or analogy. But often it is explicit, using the rational language of meditation, dialogue, or pure logic. Sometimes the poem begins by describing a scene or an experience, and then comments upon and interprets it. At other times it begins with a general idea, and then illustrates and enlarges upon it. But all of these poems, to a much greater degree than those of other contemporaries, emphasize and attempt to define their author's criticism of life. All are fundamentally philosophical or religious, even when they seem purely descriptions of nature, or love lyrics. Therefore these short poems often suggest a commentary upon the seeming irrationality and amorality of the longer, narrative poems (although usually the long poems also include passages of interpretation and criticism of their action).

The characteristic technique by which Jeffers expresses his criticism of life involves an emphasis upon perspective, or extreme distance. The poet-philosopher—whether or not he appears personally in the poem—describes the scene or experience as if from a remote distance. At the beginning of "Apology for Bad Dreams," for instance, the scene of a woman punishing a horse is described by an observer on the top of a mountain, so that both woman and animal appear "shrunk to insect size." Like Bacon's ideal observer of "Truth," the poet-spectator has retired to a hill to watch the ignorant armies clash upon the field below.

And when the poet's perspective is not described in terms of space, it is suggested in terms of time or of psychological distance. Some unusual point of view is characteristic of all these short poems.

To dramatize this unusual point of view, Jeffers has created for himself a dramatic *persona*,[1] half autobiographical and half fictional. And in this sense, these short poems share with the long ones the distinguishing techniques of myth. The poet has imagined himself as detached from the scenes and events which he describes: he has thus become in imagination his own demigod, standing above the struggle of the civilized insects. This character of "I, sadly smiling" is the self-conscious creation of the poet-artist, who has unobtrusively set the stage for a new morality play. His devil is that "monster," civilization, and his hero is the timeless American Adam. He chants once again his "song of myself," but in a new key and with modern dissonances.

The poet's imaginary detachment from his subject matter and his imaginary creation of an ideal self to dramatize this detachment are usually successful, but the result is sometimes confusing because he sometimes confuses the actual and the ideal self. Sometimes the detached self appears in the disguise of a god, wholly aloof from the struggle, who interprets it impartially. Sometimes he appears as a prophet, aloof, but passionately denouncing human folly. But occasionally he becomes involved in the struggle and loses all his ideal perspective, as in the poems written during World War II. The clearest illustration of these different aspects of the poet's *persona* may be found in Jeffers' two most successful fables: "The Humanist's Tragedy" and "Margrave." In the first, the poet does not appear, except in the character of "the god" Dionysus; in the second, he both appears as a detached observer, and speaks as a conscious moralist criticizing the actions of his characters, giving expression to his own ideal by contrast.

I *"The Humanist's Tragedy" and "Margrave"*

"The Humanist's Tragedy" describes the conflict of the rational, authoritarian Greek King Pentheus with the irrational, drunken Bacchantes, who upon a mountain are worshiping their god in obscene rites. The conflict is one of idea between the rational king who scorns emotional abandon and the irrational worshipers who scorn inhibition. "The god," however, stands aloof even from his worshipers, calling them "somewhat too drunken." When in their frenzy they imagine King Pentheus to be "a lion" and slay him, the action is presented objectively as a tragedy inevitably resulting from the conflict of overweening man with the subconscious forces of nature. "The god" is aloof, with "eyes like blue ice." And the poet's interpretation is suggested by means of ironic language describing the king—"mindful of all his dignity / As human being, a king and a Greek"—and by means of a subconscious doubt, personified as "it," which nags the king's mind. As in some of the longer narrative poems, the action seems purely dramatic, but the poet's interpretation is suggested more clearly in "The Humanist's Tragedy." Unlike "Margrave," however, the interpretation never becomes explicit, nor the language moralistic.

"Margrave" also narrates a fable to illustrate the dangers of human self-importance, but emphasizes its moral explicitly. The poem is primarily personal and philosophical, with dramatic episodes interpolated. It is the most elaborate of the many poems which describe Jeffers' "View from the Tower." It first sets the scene; then interprets the perspective which the scene illustrates (the detached observation of human folly from the remoteness of the tower beyond tragedy); then it argues against the excessive value which men attribute to human consciousness; and finally it tells a fable to illustrate the argument. The poem is complex, and the diverse elements never achieve perfect integration. But the form remains both interesting and characteristic.

The narrative episodes of "Margrave" illustrate the criticisms leveled against Jeffers' narrative poems in general: they suffer from "excess," and they are of "uneven quality." But here most obviously, they have been chosen as extreme examples of human folly. The central episode describes a youthful criminal who, partly from delusions of self-importance and partly from sadistic curiosity, has kidnaped and killed a child (much as Leopold and Loeb did). The second episode describes the reverse of the first: the youthful criminal's sister has become pregnant because of misguided pity, and his father, also driven by pity, tries to prevent some fishermen from slaughtering the sea-lions which are interfering with their sport. Both episodes illustrate the human self-importance which seeks to destroy the balance of nature.

In "Margrave" the poet speaks in many different voices and

from many different points of view. First he observes the world
from the detachment of his tower. Next he philosophizes upon
the diminished stature of man in the modern world. From this
point he argues vehemently against the excessive value which
some men still attribute to human "consciousness." Then he
introduces the story of young Margrave to reinforce his argument.
Following this extreme example of human folly, the poet asserts
his own inhumanist credo:

> . . . . I believe this hurt will be healed
> Some age of time after mankind has died,
> Then the sun will say "What ailed me a moment?"
> and resume
> The old soulless triumph, and the iron and stone earth
> With confident inorganic glory obliterate
> Her ruins and fossils. . . .

Then he reflects upon his own moral "guilt" in having helped
to spread the "contagion" of human consciousness. But he consoles
himself with the philosophic argument that man also is an
integral part of nature. Then comes the second narrative episode,
during which Margrave's father draws the analogy between
humanity and the fish which men are catching: men also are being "hooked" by the lures of human civilization. Only an aloof detachment can free man from his own folly—only this inhumanist
faith, or else death. And the poem ends with an apostrophe to
Death and a final return to the tower.

Thus "Margrave" employs most of the formal techniques
characteristic of Jeffers' short poems. Nevertheless it would fail
if it did not express its attitudes and ideas in effective poetic
language. It remains memorable primarily because of its many
passages of poetic eloquence. But this combination of poetic
skill with technical virtuosity is even better illustrated by "Apology for Bad Dreams," which has proved more popular.

II   "Apology for Bad Dreams"

"Apology for Bad Dreams," written at the climax of the poet's
fame, gives poetic expression to his "apologia," or philosophy of
life. It also expresses Jeffers' philosophy of art, which we shall
consider in the next chapter. "Apology for Bad Dreams" is divided

into four different but related sections. But it is chiefly remarkable for the vividness of its imagery and the power of its language.

The poem begins with a description of a mountain height:

> In the purple light, heavy with redwood, the slopes
>   drop seaward,
> Headlong convexities of forest, drawn in together to
>   the steep ravine. Then the ocean. . . .

But—as often with Jeffers—the static description both establishes perspective and suggests dramatic action: the slopes "drop" seaward, and the very adjective "headlong" implies violent action. The suggested violence of the action of nature which has created the scene, balances that of the human action described as occurring in the clearing below. In contrast to the impersonal violence of nature, however, the sadistic cruelty and the conscious suffering of the human violence is emphasized by "the blood dripping" and "the beast shuddering." The captivity of the bridled horse is contrasted to the "unbridled" beauty of nature. The first part ends with a biblical quotation suggesting the inhuman remoteness of God: "I create good: and I create evil: I am the Lord."

The visual contrast of mountain and clearing, as well as the ideal contrast of nature and man suggested by it, is reinforced formally by the prosodic structure.[2] The first strophe begins with long lines of approximately ten stresses each, which suggest the long perspectives of nature. Then it hurries into a series of five-stress lines, which suggest the nervous and petulant actions of man. Then it returns to the longer lines to describe the contrasting beauty of the natural scene. This formal device is repeated in later strophes. In the second, the metre contrasts the tragic beauty of the coast with the human necessity of the poet to imagine tragedies to match it. And in the fourth, the metre contrasts the more leisurely rhythms of the God of nature with the sudden violences of the God who inflicts pain and tragedy upon his creatures.

The second strophe of the "Apology" gives expression to Jeffers' psychology of tragedy, which is more Freudian than Aristotelian. Although the logic of this strophe may be questioned, the dramatic force is unmistakable, and the tormented language reflects the torment of the poet's emotion which it describes. The central

lines argue dramatically the poet's conflict with his own genius:
"I said in my heart / 'Better invent than suffer.' . . ." But the
concluding lines gradually modulate to a cradle-like metre, which
combines with its flower-petal imagery to suggest the slowing of
the pulses after violent emotional struggle:

> . . . It is not good to forget over what gulfs
> the spirit
> Of the beauty of humanity, the petal of a lost flower
> blown seaward by the night-wind, floats to its quietness.

The third strophe uses the perspectives of time rather than of
place to advance the argument. The poet remembers "the tide-
rock feasts of a dead people," who have lived and suffered here
before, and he invokes "the ghosts of the tribe." He then
generalizes: "to forget evils calls down / Sudden reminders from
the cloud. . . ." And then in his imagination the historic "ghosts
of the tribe" are joined by the ghosts of the poet's earlier
creation:

> . . . white as the half-moon at midnight
> Someone flamelike passed me, saying, "I am Tamar Cauldwell,
> I have my desire."

The actual past, which is history, and the imaginary past, which
is art, merge to realize a myth of the eternal present. And the
strange metre of the line:

> Someone | flamelike | passed me, | saying: | "I am | Tamar
> Cauldwell, | I have | my desire. | "

haunts the mind. The first half suggests by its long syllables the
slow dreaming of the spirit; the second half, the rush of the
flesh to fulfillment.

The fourth and final strophe of "Apology" repeats the earlier
comparisons and contrasts of nature and man, of the poet and
his genius, and of history and art, and then carries them to their
logical conclusions in the comparison of the poet with God:
"a man having bad dreams, who invents victims, is only the
ape of that God." But the specific word, *"that* God," also

emphasizes the interior conflict within the idea itself of God, where "He" and "I," the "spirit" and the "flesh," are ultimately identified, and God is seen to be, like man, a double agent who torments Himself in order to realize Himself. Here the language, the metre and the imagery combine to accomplish the vivid expression of the poetic idea.

III *Four Typical Short Poems*

In a sense, "Apology for Bad Dreams" consists of separate short poems dealing with four related aspects of the same idea. But Jeffers' shorter poems often differ much more completely one from another. To suggest the variety of his technique we may consider four of his short poems, written at different periods, and in different styles: "To the Stone-Cutters," one of his earliest and most famous; "Noon," written at about the same time as "Apology," but less successful; and "The Bloody Sire" and "Battle," which illustrate his later style and technique.

"To the Stone-Cutters" is remarkable in that it focuses sharply and concretely upon the ideal subject of all of his poems—the conflict of man and nature, of time and eternity. And the poem succeeds because of the sharpness of its focus and the vivid concreteness of its descriptive imagery. Its true subject is not so much the physical actions of the stone-cutters as their presumed motives: yet the physical details give reality to the ideal conflict. The poem begins by asserting this conflict: "Stone-cutters fighting time with marble"; it continues by declaring the inevitably tragic end of it: "you fore-defeated / Challengers of oblivion." But it then returns to describe the physical actions of nature which will cause the defeat of man: "knowing rock splits, records fall down, / The square-limbed Roman letters / Scale in the thaws, wear in the rain." Then the second half of the short poem draws the parallel between the physical actions of the stone-cutters and the ideal action of the poet, who "as well / Builds his monument mockingly." Only at the end is the moral made explicit: both stone-cutters and poet may achieve a relative victory in man's age-old conflict with nature. But characteristically, Jeffers has observed the activities of man from the ideal perspective of "a thousand years," and has interpreted man's conflict from that remote distance. This interpretation of experience is the true subject of the poem.

In contrast to "To the Stone-Cutters"—which describes concretely and interprets explicitly a universal, objective experience —"Noon" suggests a personal, subjective experience and interprets it more allegorically. This personal experience is that of a camper suffering the excessive heat of the noon sun in the Southern California mountains, or, more generally, that of any man suffering from the excesses of nature. The interpretation of this experience remains implicit and is suggested by the imagined role of the poet as "worshiper" of the God of nature. The subjectivity of the experience and the generality of the interpretation have made the poem less popular, but these very qualities contribute to its evocative intensity. Since Jeffers did not collect it in his *Selected Poetry*, it is reprinted in full:

> The pure air trembles, O pitiless God,
> The air aches with flame on these gaunt rocks
> Over the flat sea's face, the forest
> Shakes in gales of piercing light.
>
> But the altars are behind and higher
> Where the great hills raise naked heads,
> Pale antagonists in the reverberance
> Of the pure air and the pitiless God.
>
> On the domed skull of every hill
> Who stand blazing with spread vans,
> The arms uplifted, the eyes in ecstasy?
>
> What wine has the God drunk, to sing
> So violently in heaven, what wine his worshipers
> Whose silence blazes? The light that is over
> Light, the terror of noon, the eyes
> That the eagles die at, have thrown down
> Me and my pride, here I lie naked
> In a hollow of the shadowless rocks,
> Full of the God, having drunk fire.

Neither the scene nor the poet's position in it is particularized at first. Only the affective force of the intense heat and piercing light which he experiences is emphasized, and the relation of the poet-worshiper to this "pitiless God" is suggested. Throughout the second stanza the same blurring of focus continues as the reader's attention is directed upward to the "great hills" and as his relationship as "worshiper" at "the altars" of the

God is again emphasized. The central three lines then evoke an even more indeterminate image by means of a rhetorical question, but an image even more emotionally charged: "Who stand blazing with spread vans / The arms uplifted, the eyes in ecstasy?" The lines recall not only the religious imagery of *Paradise Lost* and of Greek myth but also the actual image of the "spread vans" of those hawks and eagles whom Jeffers has often used as symbols of the "pitiless God" of nature.

Only in the final stanza is the poet's actual position clarified in a Blake-like word-picture of the religious experience: "here I lie naked / In a hollow of the shadowless rocks / Full of the God, having drunk fire." Only by indirection has the intensity of the experience been suggested, and the religious interpretation of it clarified. But the vivid emotion remains. The poem appeals primarily to those who have shared the actual experience which it evokes and to those sensitive to the imagery of myth. But it illustrates the technique by which Jeffers suggests emotion and implies interpretation, rather than describes concretely and interprets explicitly. Other poems such as "Gale in April" successfully combine this technique of suggestion with more conventional interpretation.

A much later poem written during World War II illustrates a very different poetic technique. "The Bloody Sire" does not describe an experience concretely, nor does it evoke a subjective emotion, nor even interpret any single experience or emotion. Rather it begins with a moral judgment, and then states a philosophical proposition to justify it. Only secondarily does it illustrate the moral and philosophical idea with a series of images drawn from nature, from myth, and from history. First it uses the arguments of logic; then it convinces by means of image and analogy. It suffers, to be sure, from the poet's argumentative tone. He is answering the criticisms repeatedly leveled at him during the preceding decades—that he has unduly emphasized themes of cruelty and violence; that this emphasis is not normal but morbid and unbalanced. He is also arguing with himself against his own instinctive revulsion at the cruelties and violence of the world war. Yet the poem succeeds because of the perfection of its imagery and language and—let it be admitted—because of the perfection of its logic.

"The Bloody Sire" begins with the moral assertion: "It is not bad." And it continues: "let the bombing-plane / Speak his prodigious blasphemies." But the word "blasphemies" implies the poet's ambivalent sympathy with the very moral which, logically, he is arguing against. Then comes the philosophic proposition: "Stark violence is still the sire of all the world's values."

The following stanzas offer examples to illustrate this philosophic argument. "What but the wolf's tooth whittled so fine / The fleet limbs of the antelope?" And here the single word "whittled" suggests a multitude of meanings: it suggests the cutting of living flesh and all the resulting cruelty and suffering; but it also suggests the creation of art and the evolution of form. The God of evolution is the author of this formal beauty, but He is first the author of cruelty and violence. And the second example emphasizes a similar word and idea: "What but fear winged the birds, and hunger / Jeweled with such eyes the great goshawk's head?" The emphatic position of the word "Jeweled" emphasizes its double significance: the hawk's eye is both beautiful and cruel, just as a jewel is both shining and hard, and value attaches to both for both reasons.

The next stanza goes beyond natural examples to myth and history: "Who would remember Helen's face / Lacking the terrible halo of spears?" Once again the single word, "halo," emphasizes the ambivalent meaning; it includes both the beauty of the flesh and of the spirit, which has inspired both violence and worship. A final example then links the ideal Christ with the warlike Herod, much as Jeffers' earlier narrative poem had linked Jesus with "Dear Judas." The stanza ends: "Violence, the bloody sire of all the world's values."

The final argument of the poem is never particularized. It is merely suggested. Only the title suggests it: violence is "the bloody sire" of all the world's values, because blood and violence stain the very act of fatherhood. The first conception thus becomes the prototype of all later acts of violence. Although civilized man has sought to forget his violent origin in nature, his myth of an immaculate conception is only a dream. Violence is not morbid; it is normal. But the poem has more effectively realized this argument by means of a few vivid images and imaginative phrases than it could have done by mere logic.

A fourth short poem entitled "Battle," but subtitled "May 28, 1940," illustrates Jeffers' later technique in a different aspect. Instead of stating a general philosophic idea and then illustrating it by examples, "Battle" focuses upon a particular historic event and the experience associated with it, and then generalizes from it. The words seem prosaic and the sentences simple, but there are few more vivid descriptions of the coming war:

> Foreseen for so many years: these evils, this mon-
>   strous violence, these massive agonies: no easier
>   to bear.
> We saw them with slow stone strides approach, everyone
>   saw them; we closed our eyes against them, we looked
> And they had come nearer. We ate and drank and slept,
>   they came nearer. Sometimes we laughed, they were
>   nearer. Now
> They are here. . . .

The poem then digresses to restate Jeffers' favorite moral proposition: "It would be better for men / To be few and live far apart." But the poet suddenly recalls himself to reality: "Another dream. Another dream." Then he continues to formulate a new, realistic moral appropriate to this present reality:

> . . . we shall have to perceive that these insanities
>   are normal;
> We shall have to perceive that battle is a burning flower
>   or like a huge music, and the dive-bomber's scream-
>   ing orgasm
> As beautiful as other passions; . . .

And the poem concludes with a brief lyric which echoes the mood of the earlier "dream" but which emphasizes the new consciousness of its impossibility. Thus "Battle" includes, first, concrete description, next, moral argumentation, then prophecy, and finally reconciliation. It is not unified, nor is it wholly successful; but its very formal disunity seems to suggest the divisions and the uncertainties of the modern world.

IV *The Best Short Poems*

It is neither possible nor desirable to discuss all of Jeffers' best short poems individually. Critics and readers have chosen many different short poems as their favorites (as was also the case with the long poems). I shall simply list the more successful, popular, and interesting of these, and comment briefly on a few.

In the *Roan Stallion* volume, "Night" is outstanding.[3] Other favorites include: "Birds," "Boats in a Fog," "Haunted Country," "Shine, Perishing Republic," "Joy," "Woodrow Wilson," and "Science." Also reprinted from the earlier *Tamar* volume are: "Gale in April," "Divinely Superfluous Beauty," "To his Father," "The Truce and the Peace," "To the Stone-Cutters," and "Continent's End."

Technically, "Gale in April" is one of his most interesting poems, in that the metre suggests with great skill the tumultuous violence of its subject and the breathless excitement of the human emotions accompanying it. An interesting metrical experiment of a more obvious sort is the apostrophe "To Victory" from "The Songs of the Dead Men to the Three Dancers" in which the pounding metre echoes the rhythms of Beethoven's *Fifth Symphony* to suggest the pounding of the blood in the ears.

In *Cawdor*, "Hurt Hawks" became one of the most notorious of Jeffers' short poems, but largely because of the shock line: "I'd sooner, except the penalties, kill a man than a hawk." "A Redeemer" and "An Artist" became successful for more valid reasons (they will be discussed in the next chapter). The *Dear Judas* volume includes "Birth Dues," one of the best of those poems which describe Jeffers' religious philosophy. *Thurso's Landing* includes "Bed by the Window," an effective personal poem which Jeffers occasionally read aloud with success.

Give Your Heart to the Hawks reprints poems earlier published in a limited edition as *Descent to the Dead*. Of these, "Shakespeare's Grave" is interesting, and "Subjected Earth" is remarkable for its declaration of the poet's symbolic rejection of "the old world" of Europe. But in this and succeeding volumes the poetry becomes increasingly self-conscious and intellectual. In *Solstice*, "The Cruel Falcon," "Rock and Hawk," and "Love the Wild Swan" describe symbols vividly, but too consciously. In *Such Counsels*, "Self-Criticism in February" is effective, although argumentative in tone. From *Be Angry at the Sun* "The Bloody Sire" and "Battle" are outstanding, but they have already been discussed in detail. *The Double Axe* includes "Cassandra" and the haunting fable of doom, "The Inquisitors." And the final volume, *Hungerfield*, includes the final distinguished meditative poem on the nature of things, "*De Rerum Virtute.*"

CHAPTER 4

Philosophy and Religion

I *Nature and Man*

MORE COMPLETELY than any other modern American, Jeffers is a philosophical poet. Like the Roman Lucretius, his true subject has always been *"De Rerum Natura"*—the problem of the nature of things. Although his long poems have never been didactic, his shorter pieces have often considered philosophic problems in purely rational language. And like the poetry of Lucretius, all of Jeffers' has been deeply serious, pessimistic, and naturalistic. For the title of one of his best recent poems, he has borrowed a Lucretian phrase: *"De Rerum Virtute."*

But the philosophic poetry of Lucretius was written in an age of comparative simplicity and clarity: the "atoms" which the Roman celebrated were irreducible material facts, and the logic he used was uncomplicated by any psychology of the irrational. The later acceptance by Tertullian of religious creed *because* it was absurd would have seemed nonsense to the godless Roman poet. But Jeffers has welcomed the irrational with the rational, and has borrowed Tertullian's phrase for the title of another recent poem: *"Quia Absurdum."* Although he has rejected most of the beliefs of conventional religion, his own philosophy has never been godless, but religious in the deepest sense.

The religious nature of Jeffers' poetry has not been sufficiently recognized—probably because of his criticism of the conventional religions. But recently it has been unexpectedly emphasized by a study of the poet's vocabulary. In *The Primary Language of Poetry in the 1940's,* Josephine Miles has discovered that Jeffers uses certain key words far more often than any other major poet of his period, and that these are, typically, adjectives of position and quality. "Good," "great," "high," and "big" are his distinctive adjectives; and "man," "power," and "war" his favorite nouns. And, in general, he employs a greater proportion of adjectives to verbs and nouns than usual. His mere vocabulary reflects his concern with the relative excellence or quality of things.

But the philosophic nature of Jeffers' poetry has always been recognized. And it has constituted one of the chief attractions, and also one of the chief difficulties of the poetry. Many readers dislike all philosophy, of course; but those interested in it prefer the philosophy clear and consistent. That of Jeffers is not always either clear or consistent. It is challenging, and sometimes profound; but the poet himself has admitted its inconsistency, and has struggled throughout his life to describe his ideas more clearly.

Many critics, both sympathetic and hostile, have tried to define this philosophy. Benjamin Lehman early considered it as an attempt to see modern man as the citizen of an alien universe. Lloyd Morris examined it in terms of mysticism: "In Jeffers the heart of the ancient mystic wars with the mind of a contemporary, psychoanalytic rationalist." Hyatt Waggoner criticized it in terms of nineteenth-century science: "He absorbed without the necessary grain of salt the implications of a science that had no place for mind or values." And finally R. W. Short totally condemned "what at first seems a consistent view of life," concluding that "the philosophic content of his poems is bogus."

Some of the inconsistencies of his philosophy are conscious and intentional, necessitated by the mythical material with which he deals. Some are caused by the poetic language he uses. Many are common to the professional philosophy of his time and place: the concept of "nature" (as Professor Lovejoy has demonstrated)[1] is one of the most ambiguous, yet important, in the language. But some of his inconsistencies are personal; they result from a failure either to think through the implications of his creed or to apply them to the composition of his poetry.

Jeffers has titled his own philosophy Inhumanism, and many of his critics have described it as mere "materialism." Certainly it opposes the traditional idealistic philosophies and religions that have imagined mankind as the central concern of a personal God. But in attacking idealistic philosophy and anthropocentric religion, Jeffers has always affirmed the existence of some kind of God, or cosmic order, beyond blind materialism. Against man, he has idealized the cosmic order of nature—or, as he prefers to call it, "beauty":

> For the essence and the end
> Of his labor is beauty, for goodness and evil are two
>   things and still variant, but the quality of life
>   as of death and of light
> As of darkness is one, one beauty, the rhythm of that
>   Wheel, and who can behold it is happy and will
>   praise it to the people.

Inhumanism is a complex philosophy, involving both the poetics of tragedy and the religious experience of mysticism. But it begins with the historic philosophy of naturalism whose negative approach and whose occasional ambiguity it shares. Rather than materialism, Jeffers describes a poetic version of modern naturalism.[2]

Throughout the history of philosophy, naturalism has defined itself by opposition to some aspect of man. The Greeks contrasted nature and art. The Renaissance opposed nature to the imaginary religions of the supernatural. The Romantics opposed nature to the mechanisms of civilization. And modern naturalistic ethics opposes nature to the unnatural and the abnormal: Nature (capitalized) is the cosmic order within which natural things interact, each according to its own inner nature. All these historic aspects of naturalism have contributed to Jeffers' philosophy—and to the ambiguities of it.

Throughout his career Jeffers worked to develop an art which would transcend the traditional forms. Beginning with conventional stanzas, sonnets, rhymed couplets, odes, choruses, and all the paraphernalia of Greek and modern poetry, he progressively abandoned these forms, vowing "to shear the rhyme-tassels from my verse." In their place he attempted to develop forms directly imitating nature: the rhythms of the waves and the tides, the beat of the heart and the blood, and the verbal cadences of unconscious thought and of conversational speech. Many who dislike his naturalistic philosophy have felt that his naturalistic practice of poetry constitutes a unique achievement.

Throughout his life, Jeffers opposed all the doctrines and creeds of supernatural religion. In revolt against the traditional Christianity of his father's church, he denied the divinity of Jesus and the doctrine of the virgin birth. Beyond Christianity, he also treated Buddha and the other "saviors" as human, although often as heroic and wise. All formal religions, he believed, spring from some "private impurity" in their founders. And he denounced especially those supernatural sanctions and traditional promises which the popular religions have used to attract the credulous:

> A few centuries
> Gone by, was none dared not to people
> The darkness beyond the stars with harps and habitations.
> But now, dear is the truth. Life is grown sweeter
>   and lonelier,
> And death is no evil.

But in this attack on supernaturalism, as his critics have hastened to point out, he was grossly inconsistent; his own poetry remains full of supernatural presences, supernatural characters, and supernatural events. Throughout his career he continued to use angels and demons, alter egos and prophetic visions, immaterial ghosts and material characters returned from the grave —not only as figures of speech and psychological phenomena but as realistic actors in his dramas. How can he justify the use of supernatural beings in his own poetry, when he attacks the supernatural pretensions of traditional religions?

Clearly this inconsistency is conscious. Sometimes the poetic supernaturalism is employed for the purpose of dramatizing psychological phenomena which otherwise could only be clinically described in prose. Just as O'Neill used masks and asides to suggest the split personalities and unconscious thoughts of his characters, so Jeffers sometimes employs the supernatural to describe natural phenomena. So the induced visions of "Tamar," the alter egos and doubles of his later narratives, and the ghosts and prophetic voices which recur throughout his poems are supernatural machinery used for natural purposes.

This type of inconsistency is primarily aesthetic. If the reader is irritated by the use of supernatural means to produce natural effects, the failure is one of technique. Certainly a practice which has discarded rhyme and metre should logically discard ghosts and angels also. But sometimes the problem of dramatizing unconscious feelings in visible terms may justify the inconsistency. This technique is probably least successful when it is most conventional: for instance, several of his poems describing the

practice of poetry use "an angel" merely to personify the poetic
impulse:

> . . . the pallid
> Pursuit of the world's beauty on paper,
> Unless a tall angel require it, is a pitiful pastime.

This "tall angel" is, of course, merely a conventional phrase used
in poetic shorthand. But when a "god" or a "demon" appears to
objectify a deeply-felt impulse, which has also been motivated in
dramatic terms, the result is often effective.

The problem of dramatizing mythical events in modern terms
is often responsible for this aesthetic inconsistency. Gods and
demons were commonplace characters in ancient myth; and,
when Jeffers describes "the god" Dionysus as appearing in "The
Humanist's Tragedy" to drive his devotees mad, the mythical
characterization is entirely necessary. In "The Tower Beyond
Tragedy" this supernatural method is most successful because
the plot is most purely mythical. When the later poems "At the
Birth of an Age" and "The Inhumanist" frankly abandon naturalism for a mythical supernaturalism, the reader must accept the
obvious convention, if he reads the poems at all.

But the most troublesome intrusion of supernaturalism into
the naturalistic narratives occurs in those poems which describe
an actual "resurrection" or return of a dead man to life. The
character of Lazarus in "Dear Judas," in which the Christian
myth is most explicit and familiar, is least disturbing because
Lazarus does not act but only speaks. Nevertheless, the grave-
yard naturalism of his physical complexion and clothing remains
disturbing. Later, the short narrative poem "Resurrection" failed
almost completely because it told in flat, realistic terms the story
of a dead soldier returning from France to claim his former love,
now the wife of another. This non-mythical and unpoetic narration of a supernatural event remained flatly incredible. More
successful is "The Love and the Hate" in which the emotional
intensity of hatred which drives the dead soldier to return to
life is evoked and the gothic horror of the situation is dramatically
realized. Nevertheless, the violent revenge of a mere corpse when
dramatized in terms of realistic and purposeful action remains
incredible: the dead must work their vengeance by passive or
indirect means if they are to persuade us to a willing suspension
of disbelief.

Jeffers' most successful use of supernaturalism probably occurs when he personifies inanimate objects for purposes of fable or for poetic metaphor. Thus, the stones of Mycenae are personified in "The Tower Beyond Tragedy" in order to define the ideal of "hardness" or Inhumanism which Orestes would emulate. And "the hills" in "The Inquisitors" personify the same detached indifference to the fate of men. In this poem the poetic fable obviously does not pretend to be realistic and no mixing of genres occurs. Again, the problem is one of poetic verisimilitude only.

More fundamental, and more ambiguous, is the opposition of Jeffers' philosophy of nature to man—especially to the mechanical civilization of modern man. This is an opposition at once timely and timeless—the result at once of personal irritation and of eternal alienation.

Beginning with the industrial revolution, the romantic poets and philosophers have repeatedly denounced smoky factories, ugly cities, artificial inventions, and all the "unnatural" ways of modern living which have resulted from these mechanisms. In America the romantics have praised the frontier, the wild West, and all the "natural" life of "primitive" farmers and ranchers. And Jeffers is heir to this long literary and philosophic tradition. According to the critics' point of view, he is either the most decadent or the most powerful of the modern romantic poets. And much of his opposition to "humanity" has resulted from this historic romanticism.

But behind this romanticism, with all its emotional hatred of the evils of modern civilization, lies the scientific naturalism fathered by Copernicus. Developing gradually through the centuries, this unemotional philosophy uncentered man from his classic position in the Ptolemaic universe and exiled him to "the handmaiden planet / Of the least of the stars." Later Darwin also impugned man's ancestry by demoting him from child of God to "the bald ape's by-shot." These scientific naturalisms not only discredited all the old religions but also called into question the moralities and values traditionally associated with them. In the nineteenth century, science tended to preach a militant materialism which denied human values altogether. But in the twentieth century, scientific naturalism has attempted to define new values, which should be appropriate to man as an offspring of nature. John Dewey described these values as instrumental. But George Santayana emphasized that all aesthetic and intellectual activity was part not only of man's "nature" but also of the nature of things. Although Jeffers' attacked the traditional idealizations of man, his philosophy is much closer to the aesthetic naturalism of Santayana than to the materialism of earlier science.

Much of the inconsistency of Jeffers' philosophy derives from a confusion of the different historic varieties of naturalism. Sometimes he denounces modern man for the mechanical manner of his life which has divorced him from nature and the good earth. Sometimes he attacks all man's beliefs and ideal purposes as mere delusions—and thereby gives cause for the charge of materialism against his philosophy. And sometimes he attacks the nature of man which differentiates him from the other animals and from inanimate nature—and this attack has caused the greatest confusion. Jeffers has sometimes transferred his romantic irritation at the mechanical life of modern man and his scientific irritation at the self-centeredness of anthropocentric religions, to man himself. Yet man, as a part of nature, inevitably differs from the rest of nature.

Many of his most famous poems belong to the tradition of romantic naturalism. "Shine, Perishing Republic" contrasts "the mountains," the timeless norm of nature, with "the cities," the product of modern man. The city's "corruption," which "never has been compulsory," is caused by "the monster" of mechanical civilization. A later poem is even more specific:

> Mourning the broken balance, the hopeless prostration
>   of the earth
> Under men's hands and their minds,
> The beautiful places killed like rabbits to make a city.

And *"Ave Caesar"* speaks from the point of view of the "civilized" American:

> We are easy to manage, a gregarious people
> Full of sentiment, clever at mechanics, and we love
>   our luxuries.

But in this poem, as often, Jeffers' romantic denunciation of modern mechanical civilization enlarges into a religious denunciation of all worldly luxury. And it is this religious denunciation of worldliness which motivates the magnificent prophecy of Cassandra in "The Tower Beyond Tragedy," giving that poem —and its seemingly romantic philosophy—a timeless significance and power. Thus, the apparent exaggerations and inconsistencies of Jeffers' philosophy sometimes have their roots in a religious feeling older than philosophy itself.

Yet Jeffers' attitude toward religion was ambiguous. He, of course, always condemned not only the early religions of blind superstition but our modern civilization and its "scuttled futilities." Prophesying a "new barbarism" to follow the fall of modern civilization, he asks:

> What prophet will warn you
> When the witch-doctors begin dancing, or if any man says
> "I am a priest," to kill them with spears?

But he always respected the great religions, even while criticizing them. His early poem, "Point Lobos and Point Pinos," praised Jesus and Buddha, although it criticized their claims to ultimate truth. And his later poem "Theory of Truth" states his position even more explicitly:

> Why does insanity always twist the great answers? Because
>   only tormented persons want truth.
> Man is an animal like other animals, wants food and
>   success and women, not truth. Only if the mind
> Tortured by some interior tension has despaired of
>   happiness: then it hates its life-cage and seeks
>   further,
> And finds, if it is powerful enough. But instantly the
>   private agony that made the search
> Muddles the finding.

Basically Jeffers criticizes all religions because each preaches only a partial or "private" aspect of the truth: each exalts some single formulation of human wisdom as final. His most successful satire on this human self-importance is "The Humanist's Tragedy." In this poem the Greek religion of human reason, with its denigration of instinct, is made to appear both tragic and ridiculous. Not only the fundamentalism of traditional religion but all the religious creeds that have exalted some aspect of man at the expense of the rest of nature draw his criticism.

Yet Jeffers' own religion of "inhumanism," which opposes all the traditional religions, suffers inevitably from the same partiality, or "private impurity." If he had fully recognized and admitted his own partiality, much confusion might have been avoided. But, although his poetry has always been prophetic in tone and although his denunciations of the evils of modern civilization especially have always been personal, he has seldom admitted his partiality. The puritan-prophetic temperament from Jeremiah to Milton has never been noted for its objectivity, or sense of humor. But particularly in Jeffers' later books, where his prophecies have become most specific and his denunciations most emphatic, he asked, naïvely: "Is it necessary to add that I do not speak as one of the prophets?" His naturalistic philosophy, which declares the relativism of all religions, nevertheless prophesies its own absolute truth.

One of Jeffers' best short poems interprets his religious philosophy of naturalism, or Inhumanism, most effectively; but also suggests the basic inconsistency of it. "Woodrow Wilson" imagines a dialogue between "It" (God, or the spirit of nature) and "he" (the idealistic president, who has recently died). The poem concludes:

> "I thought", he answered,
> "That I was drawn out of this depth to establish the
> world on peace. My labor
> Dies with me, why was I drawn out of this depth?"
>
> It said "Loyal to your highest, sensitive, brave,
> Sanguine, some few ways wise, you and all men are drawn
> out of this depth
> Only to be these things you are, as flowers for color,
> falcons for swiftness,
> Mountains for mass and quiet. Each for its quality
>
> Is drawn out of this depth. Your tragic quality
> Required the huge delusion of some major purpose to
> produce it.
> What, that the God of the stars needed your help?"
> He said "This is my last
> Worst pain, the bitter enlightenment that buys peace."

In this poem Woodrow Wilson becomes the tragic hero of modern history. Wilson has been: "loyal to your highest, sensitive, brave, / Sanguine, some few ways wise." Like all men, and like all the creations of nature, he has struggled to realize his own inner nature. As a tragic hero, greater than most men, he has been motivated by "the huge delusion of a major purpose." In his self-importance he has imagined that "the God of the stars needed your help." The recognition of this delusion has become his "last, / Worst pain, the bitter enlightenment that buys peace."

But in this dialogue lurks a basic inconsistency: the "It" of the poem, and of Jeffers' whole religious philosophy of naturalism, plays both ends against the middle. And man, in the middle, never has a chance. Man is condemned by the spirit of Nature for following his own innermost nature. It is his "delusion" that he should imagine himself to be a necessary agent of Nature. "The God of the stars" does not need his help. Man should not act like a man; but, like a mountain or a star, he should strive to "cast humanity." He should strive to become an Inhumanist.

This inner confusion distorts all of Jeffers' philosophy. In "Woodrow Wilson" it is emphasized by the use of the pejorative word, "delusion." In the judgment of this hostile, Inhumanist God, man's tragic delusion is that his actions may constitute him a minor agent of God's purposes. But in the judgment of any neutral God—not anthropocentric, but still including man as an infinitesimal part of Nature—this tragic motivation would constitute an "illusion" rather than a "delusion." For in so far as man is a creature of nature, he should act according to his created nature. His illusion of purpose may, of course, lead him to tragedy and death; but, nevertheless, it remains, as Emerson called it, a "beneficent illusion." It teaches that human life is worth living and that tragic suffering may become ennobling. As part of nature, man is worth something. Only by being the thing he is—that is, by acting purposefully—can man realize his true nature.

If Jeffers' philosophy merely denied this truth—if it merely excluded man from nature, and if it denied all value and nobility to man, it would be (as it has sometimes been called) nihilistic. But actually it is ambivalent rather than nihilistic; it expresses different (frequently conflicting) points of view often within the same poem. For instance, the critique of the conflicting attitudes toward man which we have just illustrated from "Woodrow Wilson" is implicit in that poem. From the point of view of the "god of the stars" the author condemns the tragic self-importance which "deludes" man into thinking himself indispensable; but, at the same time, Jeffers values the tragic bravery

and partial wisdom which lead man to struggle to fulfill his
highest nature. Many of Jeffers' poems which denounce the
folly of man also proclaim man's relative value as "being some
ways one of the nobler animals." The poem mourning "The
Broken Balance," whose beginning we have already quoted,
concludes with the ironic question: "what, even the bald ape's
by-shot / Was moderately admirable?" And the choice of words
serves to emphasize the conflict of attitudes, whose lack of
"balance," of course, is the subject of the poem.

Logically considered, Jeffers' philosophy is inconsistent. Aes-
thetically considered, it is ambiguous—and in many of his best
poems, this ambiguity is creative. Only when the ambiguity is
unintentional and the author is passionately proclaiming some
partial half-truth is the inconsistency disturbing.

In Jeffers' poetry, Nature is always the norm in relation to
which man is measured. Man is most valued when he is most
"natural." The art of man is best when it most successfully
imitates nature, as Jeffers tries to do in his poetry. Man's religion
is best when it renounces supernatural claims. The mechanical
inventions of man have tended to alienate him from nature, and
his excessive use of the abstract intellect has had much the same
effect. But even in the modern world the norm of nature is not
unattainable: two of his best poems describe it in two of its
opposing aspects.

"Boats in a Fog" describes vividly the passage of six fishing-
boats through the offshore fog as they return to Monterey harbor
from their day's work. Their shapes become shadows in the fog,
and the muffled throb of their engines merges with the sound
of the surf. The poem ends:

> A flight of pelicans
> Is nothing lovelier to look at;
> The flight of the planets is nothing nobler; all the
>   arts lose virtue
> Against the essential reality
> Of creatures going about their business among the equally
> Earnest elements of nature.

And the sober beat of the lines emphasizes the seriousness of the
subject.

By contrast "Divinely Superfluous Beauty" describes nature

and man in their more playful aspects. Both the poem's form and its metre contrast sharply with "Boats in a Fog." The anapestic metre of the title suggests the variety of nature, while the repetition of the title suggests the identification of man with nature, even in the less earnest aspect of each: "The storm dances of gulls, the barking game of seals, / Over and under the ocean . . . / Divinely superfluous beauty." But both poems emphasize equally the value of the more "natural" activities of man—work and love—as contrasted with man's more self-conscious arts and inventions.

II *Tragedy and Beyond*

Jeffers' philosophy is often inconsistent, but the apparent inconsistencies often suggest the outlines of a deeper truth—especially in the realms of art and religion, where the apparently absurd sometimes makes the profoundest sense, if followed far enough. We consider, for instance, Jeffers' celebration of pain, which seems, as Professor Short has called it, "a wholly irrational doctrine."

Throughout his career Jeffers has repeatedly described pain and celebrated human endurance of it: "limitary pain—the rock under the tower and the hewn coping / That takes the thunder at the head of the turret—terrible and real." All his narratives have imagined violent suffering and death, and many have described this suffering so vividly that readers have often been shocked. His extreme emphasis on violence and pain and blood has even led to the charge of sadism. Any poet so obsessed by pain must seem irrational—for in rational life (as Jeffers himself has observed) "pain is a thing that is glad to be forgotten."

Although this emphasis on the doctrine of pain seems irrational, it was being celebrated by others at the time that he was writing. "Pain," wrote Edith Hamilton, "underlies the idea of tragedy." "Tragedy is nothing less than pain transmuted into exaltation by the alchemy of poetry. . . . A tragedy shows us pain and gives us pleasure thereby. The greater the suffering depicted, the more terrible the events, the more intense our pleasure. The most monstrous and appalling deeds life can show are those the tragedian chooses."[3] And "The Greek Way to Western Civilization," she writes, began with the discovery of this idea of tragedy —an art form which has always distinguished the poetry of the

Western world. The doctrine of pain thus underlies the development of modern, Western art.

But this doctrine may also underlie the modern development of Christian religion. In "Dear Judas," Jeffers imagines Jesus as consciously celebrating pain: "pain's almost the God / Of doubtful men, who tremble expecting to endure it. Their cruelty sublimed. And I think the brute cross itself . . . has been worshiped."—Earlier, in discussing this poem, we observed how Jeffers' interpretation resembles that of other modern writers, especially Yeats and D. H. Lawrence: Amos Wilder has examined the ideas of all three under the title, "The Cross: Social Trauma or Redemption?"

If this religious interpretation of the doctrine of pain suffers from the taint of abnormal psychology and "social trauma," it also suggests an alternate interpretation that lies implicit in all Jeffers' poetry. The whole religious development of Christianity may essentially be compared to the realization in history of the Greek idea of tragedy. Both Christianity and tragedy have exalted the sacrificial endurance of pain and have celebrated the "salvation" resulting from martyrdom. In this interpretation, Jesus becomes the archetypal hero of modern history. And indeed all modern history is seen as a single, composite tragic drama, whose successive protagonists have embodied in greater or less degree the idea of tragic suffering. Therefore Jeffers' ideal "Inhumanist" exclaims: "How beautiful . . . are these risings / And fallings. . . . God and the tragic poets / They love this pattern."

This conception of all human history as one tragic drama, illuminated by the human endurance of pain, serves as a kind of framework for all of Jeffers' dramatic poems. At the end of "Thurso's Landing" the poet makes the simile explicit:

> The platform is like a rough plank theatre-stage
> Built on the brow of a promontory: as if our blood had
>   labored all around the earth from Asia
> To play its mystery before strict judges at last, the
>   final ocean and sky, to prove our nature
> More shining than that of the other animals. It is
>   rather ignoble in its quiet times, mean in its
>   pleasures,
> Slavish in the mass; but at stricken moments it can
>   shine terribly against the dark magnificence of things.

Pain raises man above the slavish routine of his average existence; it gives him a nobility otherwise lacking.

This doctrine, while it approximates the ancient Greek theory of tragedy, enlarges it to the proportion of a religion or even to a philosophy of history. Man, playing his part in the tragedy of history, may through suffering become exalted beyond himself. So Lazarus praises Jesus as "one of the greatest of torchlike men," who "has chosen a painful death in order to become a God."

But if human history is the great tragedy, whose author is God, then the tragic poet becomes an imitator of God; for the poet invents little tragedies to describe to his audience the nature of life. This philosophy of art is outlined in Jeffers' famous "Apology for Bad Dreams": "a man having bad dreams, who invents victims, is only the ape of that God." Just as art is an imitation of nature, the tragic poet is an imitator of the God of nature. Tragedy teaches men that their suffering is a part of the pattern of nature. This doctrine is not irrational; it is essentially logical.

However, Jeffers has expanded with a more doubtful logic this theory of tragedy into the doctrine of vicarious suffering. In the same poem, he explains:

> I said in my heart,
> "Better invent than suffer: imagine victims
> Lest your own flesh be chosen the agonist, or you
> Martyr some creature to the beauty of the place."

That is, the tragic poet invents victims not primarily to teach the value of suffering but rather to prevent it—especially to prevent his own possible suffering:

> And I said,
> "Burn sacrifices once a year to magic
> Horror away from the house, . . ."

And so the logical doctrine of tragedy, which is primarily objective, becomes a psychological argument for the subjective efficacy of tragic invention. Aristotle gives way to Freud, with an oblique reference to the "scapegoat" theory of the primitive religions of magic. Tragedy becomes both an artistic imitation of that nature which causes man to suffer and an instrument for the circumvention of nature.

These two logically conflicting interpretations of the theory of tragedy which recur in Jeffers' poetry often cause confusion. Two poetic fables written at about the same time as the "Apology for Bad Dreams" illustrate them in different ways: "A Redeemer" leaves the choice between the two ambiguous; the companion poem, "An Artist," suggests a possible reconciliation. "A Redeemer" describes an imaginary hermit, whom Jeffers and his wife have met on a ride through the mountains. Talking with him, they observe on his hands the stigmata of wounds which have been self-inflicted. He then explains that he is trying to suffer for "the people":

> I am here on the mountain making
> Antitoxin for all the happy towns and farms, the
> lovely blameless children, the terrible
> Arrogant cities.

The poet is doubtful of the man's sanity: "I searched his face for madness but that / Is often invisible, a subtle spirit." But he is convinced by the man's sincerity and self-dedication.—Is one who courts suffering for such an imagined purpose mad, or godlike?

"An Artist" describes a similar visit with another imaginary hermit who has a different temperament. This one lives in a rock-valley which he has carved into the forms of titanic beings:

> The walls grew dreadful with stone giants, presences
> growing out of the rigid precipice, that strove
> In dream between stone and life, intense to cast
> their chaos. . . . stone fleshed, nerve stretched
> Great bodies ever more beautiful and more heavy
> with pain. . . .

The wild artist explains his purpose in carving them:

> "It is only to form in stone the mold of some ideal
> humanity that might be worthy to *be*
> Under that lightning. . . .
>
> Those children of my hands are tortured, because
> they feel," he said, "the storm of the outer
> magnificence.
> They are giants in agony. . . .
>   I have lived a little and I think

>   Peace marrying pain alone can breed that excellence
>   in the luckless race, might make it decent
>   To exist at all on the star-lit stone breast."

Unlike the hermit of "A Redeemer" this artist-hermit works only to fulfill his inner vision in artistic creation. And the poem remains unambiguous, clearly expressing Jeffers' own ideal: an artist carves a stone mountain (not unlike the Black Hills), but he creates tragic forms of his own imagining without either desiring an audience or expecting to "redeem" humanity.

In many of his best poems Jeffers has explored the problems of artistic creation and the tragic imagination. But usually his attitude has remained ambiguous. The artist is the imitator of God, but nevertheless he is also the fool of God, Who imagines his work important and therefore desires an audience or disciples. Jeffers' most anthologized poem, "To the Stone-Cutters," compares the stone-cutters to "the poet" who "as well / Builds his monument mockingly." For the poet also creates a product of only relative permanence and relative excellence. Therefore his ideal remains only "Second Best." "Best" would be not to be fooled by the "delusion of a major purpose." Speaking for himself, he admits:

>   I also am not innocent
>   Of contagion, but have spread my spirit on the deep
>   world.

And he concludes ambiguously:

>   But who is our judge? It is likely the enormous
>   Beauty of the world requires for completion our
>   ghostly increment,
>   It has to dream, and dream badly, a moment of its night.

That is, the tragic poet shares the tragic heroism of "Woodrow Wilson" and of Jesus in "Dear Judas." He desires an audience, whom he imagines he can influence, because of his delusion of self-importance. But the ideal "Artist" creates without any other purpose than satisfaction of his own impulse.

Jeffers' ideal of poetry as pure self-expression is an interesting one. But it denies the basic assumptions of tragedy, whose value lies in its expression of human purpose. Tragedy describes how men inflict pain upon one another, either to achieve power or to achieve peace, but always with the delusion of purpose. A story of unmotivated violence and purposeless suffering produces not tragic terror but sadistic horror. And the poet who denies the value of human purpose—and exactly in so far as he denies its value—shuts himself off from true tragedy.

Jeffers recognized this dilemma and sought to solve it in various ways. Tragedy is valuable, he repeats, but its value is only partial. It teaches men to recognize the nature of things and to accept pain and suffering as their lot in life:

> It is better no doubt to give crumbs than the loaf;
>   make fables again,
> Tell people not to fear death, toughen
> Their bones if possible with bitter fables not to
>   fear life.

But this value is only negative: unless the experience of tragic pain is exalted into a love of all life, including one's own pain and suffering, the result is mere stoicism. Pain must "be transmuted into exaltation by the alchemy of poetry." So long as tragic poetry is conceived merely as a kind of psychological conditioning, to toughen men's minds in their struggle for power, it exemplifies the same *hubris*—the same delusion of self-importance—which it describes. Ideal tragedy should lead to the transcendence of tragedy; it should lead men to "the tower beyond tragedy."

In his dramatic poem, "The Tower Beyond Tragedy," Jeffers suggested this ideal both explicitly and implicitly. And this poem remains one of his most effective poetic tragedies, while at the same time it denies the final value of tragedy. It fails (as some critics have emphasized) as a conventional tragedy; but it fails as tragedy in order to succeed as poetic prophecy. The traditional stories of Agamemnon and Electra are dramatized not for their own sakes but as introductory episodes to the imagined, prophetic transcendence of tragedy by Cassandra and by Orestes. The poem emphasizes from beginning to end the exaltation which tragedy may produce in the minds of men if they transcend their delusions of self-importance and renounce "Mycenae," or the ideal of power. Therefore, Orestes, who has been an actor in the earlier tragic story, becomes in the end the prophet of the poetic ideal of a love of life which includes tragic suffering, but goes beyond it.

The difficulty of "The Tower Beyond Tragedy," both as a tragic drama and as a poetic ideal, is that, in combining and fusing tragedy and mystical philosophy, it also confuses them. Orestes exclaims hopelessly: "how can I express the excellence I have found?" and the poetry, though eloquent, fails inevitably to express it clearly. Moreover, the earlier dramatic action has failed to develop the motivation—only in terms of symbol and poetic image has it been suggested. Yet the surprising fact is not the poem's failure to express the inexpressible but its relative success in suggesting that exaltation of mind and spirit which is its true subject.

The philosophic ideal of going "beyond tragedy" remains ambiguous, and two different interpretations of its are possible. Tragedy may be a necessary stage in the development of man's experience: through tragic suffering, his overweening ambition and fear of death may be transcended. This interpretation is suggested by the action of "The Tower Beyond Tragedy." Or tragedy itself, and the emotions of pity and terror involved in it, must be exorcised from man's mind: man should become Inhumanist. But then tragedy, which is a characteristically human institution and art form, must be not only transcended but rejected. This is the interpretation suggested by Jeffers' later poetry.

The ambiguity involved in these different interpretations of tragedy finds embodiment in the episode of "The Inhumanist" which describes the slaying of "the man of terrors." This shadowy figure comes as a thief in the night to the cabin of the Inhumanist hero, who

> . . . knew him and said, "My man of terrors—is it
> you? Why do you haunt me?" He chattered his
> teeth and said:
> "I am your other self. The other half of yourself,
> white of your black. I am always with you."

This "man of terrors" seems to represent the mortal anxiety which "haunts" modern man, and, as "white of your black," seeks to involve him in the tragedy of the modern world. But the ideal Inhumanist refuses to become involved and recognizes the necessity of exorcising the dangerous emotions of pity and terror from his heart. Therefore he slays his humanist self, whose face he recognizes as "his own in youth." Finally as he pushes this "self-murdered half-self" out to sea on a flaming funeral pyre, he comments that "It might be some tragic hero's death-voyage: Agamemnon's war's end . . ."

The ideal Inhumanist thus symbolically exorcises the human emotions of pity and terror, and this preserves him from rein-volvement in the tragic drama of history. But this exorcism seems to deny the efficacy and value of tragedy itself. For tragedy seeks not to destroy the emotions of pity and terror but to transmute and sublimate them. Jeffers' late reflective poetry seems to deny the value of his own earlier tragic poetry, and these contradictions, or ambiguities, confuse his doctrine of "in-humanism."

III *Inhumanism and Mysticism*

To define Inhumanism in purely logical terms is probably impossible because the word describes a general attitude which is primarily poetic and which underlies all Jeffers' poetry. This attitude was first announced in the famous passage in "Roan Stallion": "Humanity is the mold to break away from, . . . the coal to break into fire, the atom to be split." The "ism" was not officially adopted, however, until in the Preface to *The Double Axe* Jeffers used it to describe:

> . . . a certain philosophical attitude, which might be called Inhumanism, a shifting of emphasis and significance from man to not-man. . . . This manner of thought and feeling is neither misanthropic nor pessimist; . . . it has objective truth and human value. It offers a reasonable detachment as rule of conduct, instead of love, hate and envy. It neutralizes fanaticism and wild hopes; but it provides magnificence for the religious instinct, and satisfies our need to admire greatness and rejoice in beauty.

This prose definition remains paradoxical. Inhumanism is a negative word, and emphasizes *not*-man. Yet the doctrine is declared to have positive "human value," to be a "rule of conduct," to appeal to man's "religious instinct," and to his "need to admire greatness and rejoice in beauty." The obvious negative aspects of the doctrine have often been emphasized. But although the positive aspects are less obvious, they are emphasized by the poet. Since the positive aspects of Inhumanism are more poetic than logical, they need clarification in prose.

Of course every negative implies a positive: to repudiate the "excessive value" which traditional humanism puts on rationalism, decorum, urbanity, and self-restraint is also to praise the values of the instinctive life, of natural action, of simplicity and of self-expression. And Jeffers specifically praises those values of nature which are not exclusively characteristic of man. His poem "Rock and Hawk" pictures two of his favorite natural objects in one image, the falcon perched upon the rock, and exalts them as symbols of that natural life which is "inhuman."

> . . . bright power, dark peace;
> Fierce consciousness joined with final
> Disinterestedness;
>
> Life with calm death; the falcon's
> Realist eyes and act
> Married to the massive
>
> Mysticism of stone,
> Which failure cannot cast down
> Nor success make proud.

This echoes the appeal of Orestes to the stones of Mycenae for endurance and also the celebration by other poems of the wild beauty of hawks. Although endurance and fierce courage are not exclusively characteristic of man, they remain important to him.

The most characteristically "human" quality of man has always been his rationality, or consciousness. Humanism has been based upon the idea that because man thinks, he is a man and different from the beasts; and this ability to think logically has given civilized man his power over nature. But it has also set him apart from nature. Jeffers' Inhumanism has attacked this most characteristically human aspect of man exactly because it has set him apart from nature. In "The Broken Balance," he praises "the blood-loving weasel, the jewel-eyed hawk, and the tall blue heron," because

> These live their felt natures: they know their norm
> And live it to the brim; they understand life.
> While men molding themselves to the anthill have choked
> Their natures until the souls die in them.

Man's consciousness both divorces him from the rest of nature and divides him from his own "felt nature," or his inner self.

Two of Jeffers' most effective poems specifically satirize man's pride in his unique power of thought. "The Humanist's Tragedy" (which we have already quoted) uses an ironic refrain to satirize the self-consciousness of King Pentheus: "mindful of all his dignity / As human being, a king and a Greek." And "Margrave" uses a narrative framework which contrasts our "sand-grain earth" and its human inhabitants which the immensities of the stellar universe in order to emphasize the delusion of man's self-importance. Then it narrates a contemporary fable to illustrate the tragic results which may result from man's pride in rationality: "look at the fruits of consciousness." Indeed, many of Jeffers' narrative poems seem designed to illustrate the dangers of man's pride in his own powers of thought.

But this Inhumanist denial of the "excessive" value attached to consciousness by humanism also implies the positive value of those emotions of man's "felt nature" which modern civilization has most denied. Against

> . . . all the dignity of man, the pride of the only
>   self-commanding animal,
> That captains his own soul and controls even
> Fate, for a space,

Jeffers praises the instincts of the unconscious mind, which identify man with nature. In "To a Young Artist" he asserts the supremacy of these positive values:

> It is good. . . . to explore
> The peaks and the deeps, who can endure it,
> Good to be hurt, who can be healed afterward: but you
>   that have whetted consciousness
> Too bitter an edge, too keenly daring, . . .
>   . . . I tell you unconsciousness is the treasure,
>   the tower, the fortress;
> Referred to that one may live anything. . . .

Jeffers' exploration of the human unconscious may well constitute the chief philosophical contribution of his poetry. For the unconscious possesses positive values for man: it is no mere negation of consciousness. Professor Waggoner has criticized Jeffers' characters for possessing enormous "ids," but for lacking "super-egos." And, from the point of view of humanistic tragedy, the criticism is just. But the poetry of myth has always concerned itself primarily with the unconscious and irrational motives of man, and much modern literature has emphasized the values of this unconscious life. Melville praised Emerson because he loved "men who dive." And Jeffers, perhaps, "dived" more deeply into the human unconscious than any modern poet.

In exploring the depths of man's unconscious nature, Jeffers was guided partly by the traditions of myth, partly by his own intuitions, and partly by the psychological theories of Freud and Jung.[4] Although he emphatically denied the rumor that he himself was psychoanalyzed, he read widely in the literature of psychology. He sent an early copy of *Roan Stallion* to Havelock Ellis, the author of *The Psychology of Sex,* who replied with an enthusiastic letter of appreciation. Jeffers specifically affirmed the influence of Freud on his narratives of incest and on his erotic symbolism; and Jung suggested the *alter egos* and *doppelgaenger* of his narratives, together with less specific intimations of the collective unconscious and its shadowy *personae.*

But the Inhumanistic values of nature and of the unconscious derive from levels of life traditionally ranked below the human: they relate man to the beasts and to primitive, earlier cultures. Another set of values celebrated by Inhumanism relates man to the "higher" levels of life: to the transhuman universe of astronomy and to a God *not* conceived in the image of man. This aspect of Inhumanism would reconcile man to the cosmic chill of outer space and to an alien God not concerned with man's well-being.

The cosmic chill of the modern scientific world-view and the compensating values implied by it are suggested by the final lines of "Margrave":

> On the little stone-girdled platform
> Over the earth and the ocean
> I seem to have stood a long time and watched the stars pass.
> They also shall perish I believe.
> Here to-day, gone to-morrow, desperate wee galaxies
> Scattering themselves and shining their substance away
> Like a passionate thought. It is very well ordered.

Even in an alien universe certain consolations are available to man. Even in death he shares the fate of all created things, including the stars who "also shall perish." And more positively in life he shares the beauty of the stars, who also "shine their substance away like a passionate thought." He is reconciled to his fate by the realization that he shares in the cosmic order and beauty of the universe.

These values all seem reasonably clear and logical. But in attempting to imagine a God for this Inhumanist world, Jeffers has been less successful. He has vacillated between the opposing concepts of a God "not in man's form" and of a God resembling man and sharing in the human predicament, but seeking to transcend it. In "The Torch-Bearers' Race," "God . . . walks naked, on the final Pacific / Not in a man's form." But if He walks, and is naked, just how does He differ from the anthropocentric God? Jeffers' God remains ambiguous.

Jeffers' later poetry frankly accepts this ambiguity, and describes its Inhumanist God in a man's form. "At the Birth of an Age" describes "The Young Man" who combines the characteristics of Prometheus, Christ, and "The Hanged God"; and who symbolically accepts his suffering as the precondition of all existence:

> . . . without strain there is nothing. Without
> pressure, without conditions, without pain,
> Is peace; that's nothing, not-being; the pure night,
> the perfect freedom, the black crystal. I have
> chosen
> Being; therefore wounds, bonds, limits and pain;
> the crowded mind and the anguished nerves,
> experience and ecstasy.

And later the ideal "Inhumanist" also hears "a great virile cry" repeating the message:

> ". . . I am caught. I am in the net." And then,
> intolerably patient:
> "I see my doom."

Ambiguity and paradox are the lot of the Inhumanist God. Logic can go no further.

But logic has never gone to the heart of religion. The primal Jehovah also proclaimed Himself incomprehensible to human reason: "I am that I am." Religion begins where philosophy ends. And Inhumanism is a religion as much as a philosophy.

The religion of Inhumanism centers upon an experience rather

than an idea: it is poetic rather than logical. All the Inhumanist
heroes of Jeffers' poetry have celebrated the experience of
mysticism. They have not sought to know God so much as to
fall in love with Him. Beyond the consolations of philosophy,
they have described a positive "union with God," or the cosmic
order of things. And what has seemed merely an acceptance of
the inevitable, considered negatively, has become, positively, the
love of even an inhuman God. This mystical ideal of union with
God has expressed the positive aspect of Inhumanism.

Jeffers' chief heroes have specifically described and celebrated
their personal experience of union with God. Jesus emphasizes
this twice:

> He must have been lovely . . . you daughters of Jeru-
> salem that you stir not up nor awaken my love . . .
> He is lovelier than the desert dawns. Three . . . four
> times in my life I have been one with our Father . . .

And again, speaking to Judas:

> . . . I have known his glory in my lifetime,
> I have *been* his glory, I know
> Beyond illusion the enormous beauty of the torch in
> which our agonies and all are particles of fire.

And Jeffers' ideal "Inhumanist" also kneels to address the God
of nature:

> ". . . Dear love. You are so beautiful . . .
> . . . two or three times in my life my walls have
> fallen—beyond love—no room for love—
> I have been you."

But the first, and most complete description of the mystical ideal
of Inhumanism was pronounced by Orestes in "The Tower Beyond Tragedy":

> . . . how can I express the excellence I have found,
> that has no color but clearness;
> No honey but ecstasy; nothing wrought or remembered;
> no undertone nor silver second murmur
> That rings in love's voice, I and my loved are one;
> no desire but fulfilled; no passion but peace,
> The pure flame and the white, fierier than any passion;
> no time but spheral eternity: . . .
> . . . I have fallen in love outward.

Using the traditional language of mysticism, Orestes celebrated the experience of falling in love with God; but, emphasizing the non-human aspects of this God, he used the phrase "fallen in love outward."

This poetic celebration of the mystical experience is diametrically opposed to the "materialism" with which Jeffers' philosophy has often been identified. Yet it lies in the central tradition of modern American poetry and philosophy. Whitman earlier celebrated the mystical union of "Myself" with nature.[5] And Whitman's disciple, Dr. Richard Maurice Bucke, described this typically modern poetic mysticism as "Cosmic Consciousness." Later William James analyzed these poetic-mystical experiences in his *Varieties of Religious Experience*. Although Jeffers would reject the word "consciousness" in describing his mysticism, he would approve the word "cosmic." His poetry has idealized the identification of man with the cosmic order of nature by means of a mystical experience transcending reason.

To describe Jeffers' poetic Inhumanism in terms of mysticism is to suggest an explanation of many poetic attitudes which have seemed merely personal or perverse. His denunciation of humanity is repeated by many mystics who have desired to produce a "realizing sense of sin" and a resulting detachment from the affairs of this world. So Plotinus sought in the mystical experience a "liberation from all terrene concerns . . . a flight of the alone to the alone." The poet-mystic would cut humanity from his system in order to free himself to fall in love with God.

But Jeffers' mysticism, like Whitman's before him, differs from the traditional Christian and Western pattern. It approaches the mystical experience by way of the subconscious mind, and it continues to value many of the emotions of the subconscious which have traditionally been called evil. Like Whitman, Jeffers identifies dramatically with criminals and with the animals. The way to the heights lies through the depths. So his Jesus exclaims: "Life after life, at the bottom of the pit comes exultation." "The torches of violence" which burn so fiercely throughout his poetry produce no "clear, gem-like flame." They suggest also the Oriental worship of Shiva, and of the irrational gods of destruction.

This return to the subconscious values of primitive myth and to the religious values of Oriental mysticism—both of which have been suppressed or rejected by Christianity and Western mysticism—may well be justified in terms of a more comprehensive world-view. Whether this new cosmic mysticism should be described as decadent and romantic, as many critics maintain, or whether it expresses a new, non-materialistic religion implicit in the modern science of relativity and in the modern psychology of the irrational remains a matter of interpretation. The crucial question is: where does this poetic mysticism lead? If the mystical experience is idealized, what happens to the devotee who has already achieved it? What follows mysticism in time or in logic?

Throughout history, mystics who have achieved their ideal experience of "union with God" have then followed one of three courses. Some have sought to re-induce the mystical experience, and to teach others how to achieve it, like the Hindu Yogi, and the Neoplatonic philosophers. Others have withdrawn from the active world to a lonely life of passive contemplation, like the medieval hermits and saints. Still others have returned to the world of men, seeking to use their insights for the illumination of others, like most Christians and moderns. The typically Inhumanistic aspect of Jeffers' mysticism is that it seems to follow the second of these paths; it idealizes a merely passive withdrawal from the world of human history into a "tower beyond tragedy."

This tower which lies beyond tragedy, and to which the mystical experience of Inhumanism leads, is an ambiguous symbol. It suggests both the ivory tower of romanticism, which isolates the poet from the actual world, and the actual granite tower of "Tor House," from which the poet looked out upon his contemporary world. It implies both a refuge, and a place of spiritual security: it is both a "tower beyond time" (as the poet describes it), and a tower within time. Living in nature ("I entered the life of the brown forest"), the poet declares that Orestes has escaped beyond nature ("few years or many, signified less than nothing"). By going beyond tragedy, his ideal Orestes has become insulated, and isolated, from the human world of tragedy. But has he escaped into life—or from life?

Certainly the godlike isolation of Orestes is not the "reasonable detachment as a rule of conduct" which Jeffers has claimed for his Inhumanism. It is rather a total detachment—beyond humanity and beyond reason. It is an isolation which, rather than realizing nature, denies nature. Like the "delusion" of "Woodrow Wilson," this life which "signifies *less* than nothing" denies the values of that natural life which it seems to affirm. Considered by itself, this total detachment is truly nihilistic.

But "the tower beyond time" to which all mysticism leads has always been set in a dark and shadowy country. Melville so described it: "In those Hyperborean regions, to which enthusiastic Truth . . . will invariably lead a mind fitted by nature for profound and fearless thought, all objects are seen in a dubious, uncertain, and refracting light." And Hegel characterized it more succinctly as "that dark night in which all cows are black." If Jeffers sometimes loses his way in these Hyperborean regions of mystic night, he is in good company.

The mystic ideal of detachment from the world in a symbolic "tower beyond time" becomes most clear and acceptable when described in terms of time. This is perhaps the chief contribution of Jeffers' poem "The Tower Beyond Tragedy," which dramatizes the progressive attainment of the mystic ideal through a temporal and logical sequence of acts. Only after enduring the greatest tragedies life can inflict does Orestes succeed in going beyond them. Only by means of the tragic experience can human tragedy be transcended.

Jeffers' ideal of Inhumanism, as well as the poetry which gives it expression, loses power and conviction when it describes the mystic ideal only in static terms. The early narratives, especially "The Tower Beyond Tragedy," told of characters who either achieved or glimpsed the possibility of this superhuman ideal. "Dear Judas" separated the mystical experience (achieved by Jesus) from the post-mystical ideal of Inhumanism (suggested verbally by Lazarus), but it implied their sequence in terms of time and of logic. The later poems mostly described protagonists incapable of even imagining transcendence. "At the Birth of an Age," like "Dear Judas," did suggest this transcendence in terms of sequence, but it dissociated the earlier human acts from the later superhuman ones. And "The Inhumanist" described only the timeless inhuman ideal, suggesting the earlier tragic and mystic experiences by means of allegorical episodes such as that of "the man of terrors."

CHAPTER 5

"The Atom to be Split"

JEFFERS' POETRY contains many logical contradictions, as we have seen. Yet, of course, Jeffers has not written philosophy but poetry. And poetry has never been subject to the laws of logic: like all imaginative literature, it suggests ambiguous truths and arouses contradictory emotions by the non-logical methods of myth, analogy, and metaphor. The earlier chapters have analyzed Jeffers' long poems in terms of myth, and his short poems in terms of perspective and form. In this chapter, I shall develop the implications of a single metaphor to suggest the multiple meanings of his poetry.

"Humanity," Jeffers wrote in 1925, "is the atom to be split." In "Roan Stallion" he used this metaphor to suggest the meaning of this poem, and, perhaps, of all his future poetry. But the meaning is neither simple nor immediately apparent. This master metaphor suggests the analogy between the smallest unit in physical nature, the atom, and the smallest unit in human nature, the human individual. Each is apparently indivisible, yet each is subject to division. The splitting of each may be violent, but will release unsuspected reserves of energy. This violence may be destructive, but it will also lead to new discoveries, as well as to the potential harnessing of this energy. In 1925 the possibility of splitting the physical atom had been recognized, and at that time constituted the immediate goal of physical science. Jeffers suggested that a similar achievement might also be the goal of imaginative literature, and of his own poetry in particular. Tragedy, as he conceived it, was a means to this end: "Tragedy that breaks a man's face and a white fire flies out of it . . . inhuman science, / Slit eyes in the mask."

This metaphor also suggests a possible explanation of Jeffers' philosophy of Inhumanism, and of his poetic theory and practice; yet at its base lies a logical paradox and ambiguity. "Humanity" is the explicit object of the metaphorical statement, and of the physical action prophesied by it. But "humanity" is also the implied subject of the statement and the chief actor in the drama prophesied. Ambiguously, humanity is both the natural object and the superhuman subject. And this metaphor—suggesting the identity of man with nature, on the one hand, and of man with the God who creates and destroys nature, on the other hand—denies the central, humanistic value of man.

In Jeffers' poetry, man ceases to exist as an autonomous human individual, independent of nature or of God. Rather he appears in two new roles. First, he is a natural object, motivated by the forces of nature: in the narrative poems he often becomes the personification of natural force and is possessed by the demonic drive of his natural instincts. Second, man appears in the roles of a godlike observer of human folly and of an ideal actor in the cosmic drama: in the short poems he watches the insect-like human beings from godlike perspectives, and criticizes their actions as a tragic poet—"the ape of God." But these two roles, of natural object and of godlike subject, are contradictory to each other, and to the traditional humanistic view of man (note how the phrase "the ape of God" denies the very idea of humanism), and these contradictions cause confusion.

By traditional standards, therefore, Jeffers' poetry is illogical and inhuman. It is ambiguous in meaning and ambivalent in feeling. By means of myth and metaphor it implies not only that man must live with this ambivalence but that he may even use it for creative purposes. Objectively, in his role as godlike discoverer, man may use his own suffering to unlock the secrets of the universe. And subjectively, he may use his knowledge of the nature of things to comfort himself in his own tragic predicament in nature.

"Humanity is the atom to be split." And that "ape of God," the tragic poet, is the divine agent who may accomplish this splitting of the atomic human consciousness. Like the scientist who is also an agent of God, man may transcend his own human nature and imagine the destruction of humanity, and perhaps learn power and wisdom thereby. The analogy between atomic scientist and tragic poet lies at the heart of Jeffers' poetry. No longer is "the poet" the mere aesthetic observer of sunrises; he becomes a discoverer of psychological truths, and even an agent in the harnessing of human power.

In the metaphor, if we follow it further, humanity resembles the physical atom. Seemingly unified and stable, man is composed of many unstable elements. When these elements are subjected to sudden and violent pressures, they may disintegrate in sudden explosions. By isolating the most unstable elements in humanity and subjecting human individuals to violent pressures, the tragic poet may bring about such human explosions. These explosions may cause the disintegration or death of the individuals concerned; but they will also cause the release of immense reserves of human energy, accompanied by flashs of illumination. These explosions may light "the torches of violence."

This second metaphor in turn suggests new meanings. Violence, although destructive, may bring illumination. The destruction of the unstable human atoms may illuminate the nature of human history. These "torches of violence" also suggest a kind of ritualistic procession through history in which the destruction of men and of civilizations may mark the progress of The Torch-Bearers' Race. But "the torches of violence" are smoky, their light often murky. The tragic poet who splits the human atom to light these torches deals with dangerous materials, and his meaning also may remain dark.

A letter written by Jeffers in 1932 emphasizes explicitly the analogy between the tragic poet and the atomic scientist:

> . . . hate perhaps more than love needs energy; certainly pain more than pleasure makes explosions of energy; though of course it burns it up sooner. . . . I think one of the most common intentions in tragic stories, from the Oedipus down, is to build up a strain for the sake of the explosion of its release,—like winding up a ballista.[1]

On the primary level, the tragic poet seeks to create mere explosions of human energy, but he hopes secondarily to illuminate human psychology and history.

The "Prelude" to "The Women at Point Sur" develops this analogy in poetic language. It compares the physical energy stored in the oil-tanks of Monterey with the human energy of the characters—both to be released by "lightning":

> . . . The oil-tank boils with joy in the
> north. . . . (it) roars with fulfilled desire,
> The ring-bound molecules splitting, the atoms dancing
> apart, marrying the air.

Explicitly in the narrative poem that follows, the Reverend Barclay emphasizes his purpose "to burn the world down to significance." But the deluded hero fails in his demonic quest for illumination through violence, and the poem fails with him. The little human explosions which he sets off fail to produce the illumination for which he hopes.

In "The Women at Point Sur," however, the hero makes an almost casual remark which suggests a possible explanation of his own—and his author's—dilemma: "The American mind short-circuits by ignoring its object." In the process of creating a series of explosions of the human consciousness, the tragic poet may fail to light the "torches of violence," and the illumination which should follow tragedy may fail. "The American mind short-circuits" when it ignores the fact that humanity belongs to two different circuits, or worlds: to the chaos of nature; to the cosmos of God. The illumination of human meaning will be achieved only when the poet creates characters who belong to both worlds and who remain conscious of the fact.

The most damning criticism of Jeffers' narrative poetry has emphasized that his characters often seem mere automatons who are compelled by blind instincts and unconscious desires, wholly unable to guide or govern themselves. Facing tragic situations, they seem to go into cataleptic trances, to act without volition or conscious choice. And their narratives increasingly resemble that old art-movie "The Cabinet of Doctor Caligari" in which a mad scientist drives his trapped victims like Pavlov's dogs through meaningless mazes. Their blind tragedies develop only in one dimension because the protagonists exist only on one level—that of animal nature. When men are unable to act or to think as human beings—and, more important, when they ignore their relationship to the God of nature whose creatures they are—their tragedies become meaningless; "the torches of violence" gutter out, smothered in their own smoke.

But this criticism of meaningless violence does not apply to most of Jeffers' narrative poems. Tamar, for instance, has been accused of blind compulsion; but in "Tamar," although the heroine acts out a predetermined drama of incest, she remains acutely conscious of the moral implications of her actions, and she emphasizes them explicitly, and repeatedly. In "Roan Stallion," also, the heroine achieves significance because she is torn by confused loyalties; she is compelled by her human loyalty to

shoot the wild stallion, and thus symbolically to "kill God."
Jeffers' narrative poems written between 1935 and 1945 are
subject to the criticism of automatism and meaninglessness. But
the excellence of his later allegorical narratives lies in the fact
that they consciously contrast the senseless violence of animal
man to the ideal morality of their Inhumanist heroes, or gods.

Much of the difficulty of Jeffers' poetry is caused by this
problem of the double nature of humanity. Man is both animal
and poet-scientist—both the object of God's anger and the agent
of God's purposes. Objectively, humanity is the atom to be
split; but, subjectively, humanity is also the agent who subjects
himself to the violation of war and of tragedy. By nature an
animal, man is by potentiality a god. But when Jeffers damns
"humanity," he remembers the driven human animal.

This confusion of man the object and man the subject is both
emphasized and partially explained in the final section of
"Apology for Bad Dreams" in which the poet "apologizes" for
his own dilemma as writer of tragedy:

> He brays humanity in a mortar to bring the savor
> From the bruised root: a man having bad dreams, who
>   invents victims, is only the ape of that God.
> He washes it out with tears and many waters, calcines
>   it with fire in the red crucible,
> Deforms it, makes it horrible to itself: the spirit
>   flies out and stands naked, he sees the spirit,
> He takes it in the naked ecstacy; it breaks in his
>   hand, the atom is broken, the power that massed it
> Cries to the power that moves the stars, "I have come
>   home to myself, behold me.
> I bruised myself in the flint mortar and burnt me
> In the red shell, I tortured myself, I flew forth,
> Stood naked of myself and broke me in fragments,
> And here am I moving the stars that are me."

But let us translate this poetry into prose: "He"—that is, God—
"brays humanity in a mortar"; that is, He crushes and kills
individual men. But "a man having bad dreams"—that is, a
tragic poet—does the same thing in imagination. "He"—now, God
and tragic poet combined—makes humanity "horrible to itself,"
so that "the spirit" will "fly out and stand naked"—that is, will
separate itself from the flesh. When the human "atom is broken,"
"the spirit" will identify itself with God, or "power," and will

cry out: "I have come home to myself." But "the spirit" will also remember the flesh: "I tortured myself . . . and broke me in fragments." Because of the self-torture of man by man "here am I moving the stars that are me." Paradoxically, man's inhumanity to man has given him not only power over nature but also understanding of himself. Man's inhumanity, in his double role of divine agent and natural object, has achieved for him super-human power and knowledge—therefore, Inhumanism.

But other ambiguities and confusions remain. Man, in his role of scientific discoverer and tragic poet, is potentially an agent of God. But man the creative scientist and poet may forget or ignore this role of agency, and may even imagine himself to be God. Thus, the psychological horror aroused by the figure of the mad scientist—the Dr. Caligari, who tortures his victims without apparent purpose or reason. And thus the failure of the Reverend Barclay in "The Women at Point Sur," who confuses his godlike quest for ultimate truth with his human quest for power and self-gratification. And thus the failure of the poem with him, for it did not clearly distinguish his madness from the heroism of his quest. Later, in "Margrave," Jeffers imagined a mad young scientist as his extreme example of human depravity; and, because he made the madness clear, the fable also came clear.

Yet the mere fact that man is a double agent necessarily involves him in ambiguity and confusion: this ambiguity is essential to the nature of man. In his role of poet-prophet, Jeffers has also suggested this inevitable ambiguity. His fictional inhumanist, who tortures himself in order to discover himself, also shadowed forth the actual dilemma of the modern nuclear scientist who faced the ultimate implications of his discoveries. Knowing that his godlike power might be used for the destruction of humanity, this scientist recognized his inner ambivalence. So Robert Oppenheimer, observing the first nuclear explosion at Los Alamos, recalled the ambivalent wisdom of the Hindu scriptures: "*I am the creator and the destroyer of worlds.*" And this actual ambivalence of the historic scientist—the human agent of God, yet also the potential object of the wrath of God—had earlier been prophesied by the modern poet. "Humanity is the atom to be split"—both in poetic imagination and in prophetic actuality.

Jeffers' poetry reflects these ambiguities of the modern world. Both his fictional characters and his personal poems sometimes become confused by this ambiguity, and they dream nightmares such as "The Women at Point Sur." But often Jeffers, like his mythical Cassandra, realistically prophesies the actual nightmare of modern history, and then his very ambiguities seem to clarify our actual confusions.

In many different senses, Jeffers is the poet of the Atomic Age. His long narrative poems consciously build up physical and psychological pressures upon his unstable characters until violent explosions result. The impact of these upon the reader's consciousness is often great; and, judged by the simple standards of sensation, the best narrative poems are extremely powerful. But beyond sensation, Jeffers' poetic explosions of the human consciousness often release psychic energy and produce intellectual illumination. At best this released energy induces an extraordinary exhilaration, and the sudden illumination opens up new insights. Yet beyond both sensation and illumination, Jeffers' poetry prophesies—and in the deepest sense. It shadows forth the historic ambiguities and the actual dilemmas of the scientist and the poet of the Atomic Age. His denunciations of man and his prophesies of doom both foreshadow, and are shadowed by, the mushroom cloud.

Jeffers may be described as the poet of the "big bang." At the opposite pole from T. S. Eliot, who prophesied "This is the way the world ends, / Not with a bang, but a whimper," Jeffers both prophesies and in a sense produces the bang. He is the poet of Armageddon and the prophet of doom. And after his poetic explosions have occurred, he is not interested in the whimpers.

At its best, the emotional impact of his poetry is very great. Its sudden flashes illuminate the nature of modern man. But—to develop further the analogy between tragic poet and nuclear scientist—his poetry deals with dangerous materials whose laws are not fully understood. His explosions of the unstable human consciousness have released poisonous products of mental fission. After the releases of power and the flashes of insight, the dissociated emotions and ideas have sometimes produced a kind of psychological fallout. In the poetry of his middle period, Jeffers dealt with these schizoid materials, and the poetry suffered. In the middle of "The Women at Point Sur," he recognized that "these [idols] have gone mad." Later the characters of "Solstice" and "Such Counsels" seemed to recognize their madness from the beginning. Therefore readers and critics have instinctively rejected these poems because of the dangerous nature of their materials and the author's lack of control over them. As the psychological fallout descended, the critic-monitors sought to sink this poetry into the sea of oblivion.

"Humanity is the atom to be split": the metaphor suggests both the nature of Jeffers' poetry and a source of its power. The early poems, which won wide fame, still retain their power and their dark beauty. Although the poems of the middle period lost much of this, and dealt with dubious materials, they sometimes developed the author's thought to suggest the ambiguities of the modern world; like the unpopular fables of Melville's later years, they still open up endless avenues of speculation. Jeffers' later fables and allegories prophesy the doom of modern man, but—like all veritable prophecies— they also comfort by recalling the long perspectives of myth and of history.

CHAPTER *6*

Conclusion

OVER THE YEARS Jeffers' reputation—both critical and popular—has fluctuated more than that of any contemporary author. Moreover, the quality of his poetry has varied greatly in the course of his long career. Even the philosophic meaning of it has been subject to reinterpretation—both by the author and by his critics. It would be rash to prophesy what the verdict of posterity will be; yet his poetry itself has often attempted to prophesy: "O vulture— / Pinioned, my spirit, one flight yet, last, . . . unguided, / Try into the gulf." And criticism, like prophecy, is (or should be) a revelation of the essential nature of things. What is the essential nature of Jeffers' poetry?

The one quality of his poetry upon which most critics have agreed is its "power." At best it appeals immediately to the reader's imagination and arouses powerful emotions. It not only narrates actions whose impacts are powerful and describes scenes of spectacular grandeur but it conveys the intensity of these actions and the majesty of these scenes in words and metaphors of great power. Of course these actions are often brutal, the scenes inhuman, and the emotions aroused disturbing and shocking, but at its best, the affective power of this poetry is great.

This power is, in a sense, elemental. It springs in part from the very nature of Jeffers' subject matter: his narratives deal with the elemental emotions of man and his descriptions with the primeval landscapes of nature. Both in fact and in imagination he is poet of the American West whose wildness and spectacular grandeur he has celebrated. Indeed, the nature and the impact of his poetry have been compared to that of the actual Grand Canyon.[1] Like the Grand Canyon, his poetry arouses the emotions of terror and awe, and suggests magnificence. But also like the Canyon, it lacks all the modulations and subtleties characteristic of the normal landscapes of the world. It deals only with the uncivilizable aspects of life and suggests the abyss that lies always at the foot of modern man. As tourists and critics alike have pointed out, one grows tired of gazing only at the Grand Canyon.

In the realm of literature, this quality of Jeffers' poetry may be compared with that of the Elizabethan Christopher Marlowe. Like Marlowe, Jeffers has dealt with the extremes, not the norms, of human emotions; both poets have described unrelieved violence and inhuman cruelty, pure sensuality and the primal lust for power. Like Marlowe, Jeffers has manifested the gift of verbal magnificence in describing these. Like Marlowe also, he carried this gift to the verge of extravagance: the poetry of both is full of "purple passages." If Jeffers never equalled Marlowe's immortal "Was this the face that launched a thousand ships?" he imagined for his Helen "the terrible halo of spears." Readers of Jeffers' poetry are often struck by the mere evocative power of the phrases and metaphors. At its best, his poetry does approach that of Marlowe in its raw power and in its verbal magnificence.

If this praise seems extreme and this criticism subjective, it may also suggest the limitations of Jeffers' poetry. Like Marlowe, Jeffers lacks all the variety and subtlety of a poet such as Shakespeare. Indeed, poets like Marlowe and Jeffers seem to gain their emotional intensity by their very exclusion of those shades and subtleties which describe "humanity" in all its fullness. As a freshman in college, for example, I argued with my father that Marlowe was a much greater poet than Shakespeare, and something of this adolescent enthusiasm for the unrestrained emotions and the rhetorical excesses of Marlowe probably predisposes to an enthusiasm for the similar defects of Jeffers.

"Expression is what we want," exclaimed Emerson, "not knowledge, but vent." Jeffers, in the tradition of Emersonian individualism, has developed the power of pure expression to a high degree. His ability to combine mere words in effective patterns is impressive. His metaphors are imaginative, and they open avenues of suggestion and analogy. His poetic rhythms and cadences are both original and varied. His long, free, narrative verse-line is perhaps his most original technical invention. The myths which he has imagined for his narratives are often unique, even when they seem to imitate the classic patterns. His poetic prophecies are impassioned. His poetic and dramatic techniques combine an appeal both to the popular and to the critical reader. His poetry has given expression to the subconscious anxieties of modern man; and, if these have seemed exaggerated and unacceptable, at least—in Emerson's phrase—he has given them "vent."

Jeffers' gift of purely verbal expression is easy to illustrate—many phrases quoted in earlier chapters might serve. Sometimes his phrases follow conventional metrical patterns, as in the title "Divinely Superfluous Beauty." Often they bear a colloquial accent of their own: "corruption / Never has been compulsory." Sometimes the mere sound of the words magnifies their meaning: ". . . and the earth / With confident inorganic glory obliterate / Her ruins and fossils." Sometimes this verbal magnification approaches exaggeration: "cliffs of peninsular granite engirdle." But always the words and phrases give expression to their emotions and ideas by means of a consciously heightened verbal artistry.

Jeffers' metaphors are sometimes spectacularly expressive. Some of the meanings latent in his most famous metaphor—"humanity is the atom to be split"—have been developed in Chapter V. But often the poet himself has elaborated some simile, toward the end of a narrative poem, in order to illustrate and to emphasize the meanings of it. His comparison of the aspiring spirit of man to the spawning salmon which struggles "to find its appointed high place and perish" concludes "The Loving Shepherdess"; and his final simile in "Dear Judas" is perhaps even more effective. Addressing Judas, Lazarus prophesies:

> . . . your name shall couple
> With his in men's minds for many centuries: you enter
> his kingdom with him, as the hawk's lice with the
> hawk
> Climb the blue towers of the sky under the down of
> the feathers.

The final simile "as the hawk's lice with the hawk" may be disturbingly ugly—like so much else in Jeffers—but it is perfectly meaningful. And its very ugliness seems to right the balance of the poem—to correct the initial emphasis on pure love suggested by the title "Dear Judas." Although Jesus loved "dear" Judas, the traditional values remain true: the spirit of the one is like that of the hawk climbing the sky, but that of the other like the ugly parasite upon him. Only the phrase "the blue towers of the sky" seems self-consciously rhetorical.

The metres and the rhythms of this poetry also contribute to its power of expression to an unusual degree. Going beyond the traditional forms and patterns of English poetry, Jeffers has developed his own "free" rhythms. These imitate both the natural rhythms of speech and the actual rhythms of nature rather than the regular iambics of blank verse or of the couplet. Thus the first lines of his poem, "Night," seem to echo the actual rhythms of the ebb tide which they describe by means of their verbal cadences:

> ˘ — — ˘ ˘ — ˘ — ˘
> The tide slips from the rock, the sunken
> — — — ˘ — ˘
> Tide-rocks lift streaming shoulders
> — ˘ ˘ —
> Out of the slack. . . .

Where the first and third lines approximate conventional rhythms, the second line imitates the slow, non-rhythmical emergence of the tide-rocks from the ocean ebb by means of its own slow, consonant-clotted syllables which simply cannot be pronounced rapidly. The second stanza of this same poem uses a longer line and a different metre to suggest the slowing of the pulses of life after the coming of night:

> — ˘ ˘ — — ˘ — ˘ ˘ — — —
> Over the dark mountain, over the dark pinewood,
> — ˘ — — — ˘ ˘ — ˘ — ˘ — ˘
> Down the long dark valley along the shrunken river,
> ˘ — ˘ — ˘ — ˘ —
> Returns the splendor without rays, . . .

Equally expressive and equally natural is Jeffers' long, narrative verse-line. In contrast to the shorter lines of his descriptive and lyric poetry, his long lines reproduce the rhythms of speech—in order to suggest the oral narration of traditional myth and fiction —at the same time that they maintain formal control over their material. The concluding lines of "The Tower Beyond Tragedy," printed on the page opposite the poem, "Night," illustrate this free narrative verse, with its irregular long lines of ten accents each:

She túrned and éntered the áncient hóuse. Órestes

wálked in the cléar dáwn; men sáy that a sérpent

Kílled him in hígh Arcádia. But yóung or óld,

few yéars or mány, signified léss than nóthing. . . .

This conscious artistic technique, designed carefully to disguise its artistry, is immediately expressive and constitutes an original development in the technique of modern prosody which criticism has not yet adequately recognized.[2]

At its best, Jeffers' verbal magic, his metaphoric imagination, his metrical skill, and his prosodic originality combine to make his poetry remarkably expressive. Negative criticism of this poetry has focused almost entirely upon what he expressed. This includes all those myths, fictions and tragedies which he described objectively in his longer poems. It includes those ideas, moral judgments, and personal attitudes which he has expressed subjectively in all his poems.

The essential nature of Jeffers' narrative poems has never been recognized clearly—even, I think, by the poet himself. Usually these long poems have been called tragedies. They have been produced on the stage as tragedies, they have been criticized for their imperfect success as tragedies, and the poet himself has described some of them as tragedies. Yet they have always diverged from the strict patterns of classical tragedy. Moreover, they have changed over the years both in nature and in quality. Beginning as myths, they occasionally approximated the tragic patterns. But gradually they changed to become psychological melodramas or supernatural fantasies, and they ended as religious allegories. The uncertain and changing nature of these poems, as well as the uncertain and changing attitude of the poet toward them, has contributed to the confused rejection of them by some modern critics.

Classical tragedy always described actions of a certain magnitude and heroes of a certain nobility—the mere importance of the protagonists emphasized their significance to the classical audience. Modern tragedy, however, has often described the less heroic actions of less important characters. Nevertheless the modern tragedian has persuaded his audiences of the significance of these less heroic characters by showing the inner identity of their emotions and struggles with our own. And all tragedy, whether classical or modern, has emphasized this universal significance by means of some "recognition scene" in which the hero consciously recognizes his own tragic flaw and then consciously confronts his own fate. This recognition by the tragic hero of the nature of things and of his own necessary involvement in it has distinguished tragedy, both ancient and modern, from melodrama and from fantasy.

The heroes of Jeffers' narrative poems have approximated the traditional, classical patterns of tragedy only occasionally, when they have followed the classical myths, or (as in "Dear Judas") actual history. Nevertheless, all the heroes of Jeffers' earlier narratives did realize, to some degree, the patterns of modern tragedy. Tamar did learn to recognize and to accept the ultimate evil of her own nature; California did recognize the divisions of her own loyalty; and "The Faithful Shepherdess" remained faithful to her own impulsive nature to the tragic end. All Jeffers' earlier protagonists, that is, achieved conscious recognition of their relation to the nature of things, and confronted their fate like human beings, in spite of their own evil, divided, or undisciplined natures.

But when Jeffers began to write "The Women at Point Sur," the pattern changed. The new protagonists seemed to lose sense of their identities or relations, and the poet recognized this fact and proclaimed the failure of these "new idols." Nevertheless he confidently prophesied the ultimate success of his future, tragic heroes. Moreover, this prophecy defined clearly the essential nature of his tragic purpose:

> . . . I sometime
> Shall fashion images great enough to face him
> A moment and speak while they die.

This is an almost perfect statement of the universal ideal of the tragic author. His earlier heroes had achieved something of this moral courage and tragic consciousness, but his later heroes never approached it.

The failure of all Jeffers' later narrative poems to achieve that tragic ideal which he had so clearly described and so confidently prophesied for them is, I think, a major failure. After "Dear

Judas" and "The Loving Shepherdess" his heroes gradually lost their courage of action, or else their clarity of mind. Progressively they became the blind, driven creatures of their instincts, or else the inactive spectators of the human tragedy. Either they forgot their human sense of relationship to the nature of things, so that they became unable to "face him and speak" while they died, or they retired from all human tragedy to become hermits, and to "face him and speak" freed from the agony of dying. In either case, his narrative poems ceased to be tragic; they became either unconsciously melodramatic, or self-consciously allegorical.

But if Jeffers' long poems have never been tragedies in the strict, classical sense and if they have become less tragic over the years, they have realized other qualities. As we have seen, these long poems have created modern myths. And all Jeffers' poems have shared the nature of religious prophecy. Like the biblical prophets of old, he has imagined the destruction of the civilization in which he has lived; and like the author of Revelation, he has symbolically revealed its doom. But unlike the biblical prophets, he has prophesied from the secular perspectives of world history.

Like "Shine, Perishing Republic," many of Jeffers' best poems have been pure prophecy. His first successful volumes concluded with "Continent's End" and "The Torch-Bearers' Race." His long poems also have developed this element of prophecy; "The Tower Beyond Tragedy" centered upon the eloquent prophecy by Cassandra of the rise and fall of all the empires of the earth, ending with the imagined return of the ice age: "O clean, clean, / White and most clean. . . ." But by means of symbol and metaphor even his most objectively imagined myths and fictions have also prophesied the doom of an introverted humanity which blindly seeks power over its fellow men.

In its pure form, Jeffers' prophetic poetry has repeated the . religious anti-materialism of the older prophets. "Where are prosperous people my enemies are," exclaims Cassandra; and her denunciation ends with: "A mightier to be cursed and a higher for malediction"—the arch-materialist, America. This poetry has given modern expression to the essentially religious, and ultimately Oriental, distrust of all material luxury. It gives voice to the anguished cry of the rich man seeking to go through the eye of the needle.

But Jeffers' poetry is seldom purely religious or purely prophet-

ic. It usually shares the Greek sense of tragic involvement in man's
political struggle for human freedom, and derives much of its
prophetic power from its own involvement in the American con-
tinuation of this dream of political freedom. This poetry also
gives voice to the lamentations of the historic American dreamer
who is beginning to realize that "These dreams will not be
fulfilled." In 1929 Jeffers stood "at the peak of time" and
prophesied the failure of the historic American dream.

Considered as prophecy, his poetry derives its tension from
the author's lifelong involvement in this historic American idealism. During World War I—as Mrs. Jeffers has recorded—he
underwent a conscious counter-conversion from the naïve Wil-
sonian idealism of making the world safe for democracy. His
first—and perhaps his best—mature volume of poetry expressed
this prophetic pessimism, and his poems "Woodrow Wilson" and
"Shine, Perishing Republic" gave it classic expression. These
poetic prophecies became "classic," however, because they realized the essential nature of prophecy, and revealed the universal
necessity behind the particular event.

As his mythical Clytemnestra had exclaimed to Cassandra,
"You are prophesying: prophesy to a purpose, captive woman."
Jeffers' own late poetry attempted to prophesy to a purpose.
Having foretold the destructive nature of imperial power, he
allowed himself to become captivated by the patriotic hope of
preventing that very future whose nature his earlier prophecy
had revealed. When this hope failed, and his reinvolvement with
political idealism led to frustration and despair, he sought total
disinvolvement from the tragedy of his time. In poetic imagination, he sought to create his ideal "Inhumanist."

In the last analysis, all Jeffers' poetry leads toward this philosophic or religious attitude of "Inhumanism"; and most readers
have criticized the poetry because of this philosophic attitude.
Many have been disturbed by the ambiguities involved in it,
or have been repelled by the apparent nihilism of it. Others,
challenged by the originality of this new philosophy, have felt in
it a positive appeal to the religious instinct for solitary com-
munion with the God of nature. In any case, the poet's intense
and single-minded devotion to this imperfectly apprehended and
unpopular ideal has inevitably limited his audience—at the same
time that it has strengthened his appeal to it. Whatever the
judgment of posterity may be, many will never enjoy Jeffers'

poetry, but some will continue to be fascinated by it. This is in the nature of all violently tragic and prophetic literature of the extreme type—like that of Marlowe and of Jeremiah, to name only the classic exemplars.

Even in its formal aspects, Jeffers' poetry has been conditioned by his underlying philosophic and religious attitudes. Literature which deals with the extremes of human experience and with the ultimates of human thought sometimes achieves its greatest success by means of its own apparent formal imperfections. Its dual form may emphasize its emotional ambivalence and its logical discontinuity. Some of his poems fail as tragedy in order to succeed as prophecy, and others fail as realistic narrative in order to succeed as symbolic myth. But, of course, some also fail because of the author's uncertainty of intention.

Many of Jeffers' poems have achieved distinction for many different reasons. No single poem, long or short, can be singled out as certainly his best. One quality, however, distinguishes all those poems which different readers have most admired and different critics have most praised. All his best poems include striking passages of poetic eloquence or imaginative beauty. The qualities of verbal magnificence, of metaphoric imagination, and of originality of expression distinguish his poetry. To an unusual degree, he possessed the power of pure expression. This is not so common a gift as to be easily forgotten.

Notes and References

Chapter One

1. All bibliographical references in this chapter are to L. C. Powell, *Robinson Jeffers*, or S. S. Alberts, *A Bibliography of Robinson Jeffers*, unless otherwise specified.
2. See Edith Greenan, *Of Una Jeffers*.
3. George Santayana, *The Winds of Doctrine* (New York, 1926), p. 213.
4. These and other youthful poems and prose pieces were collected in Alberts' *Bibliography*.

Chapter Two

1. Yvor Winters, *In Defense of Reason* (New York, 1947), p. 582.
2. "Preface to 'Judas,'" in *The New York Times*, drama section (October 5, 1947). This preface has not been reprinted.

Chapter Three

1. George B. Kiley, in his dissertation *Robinson Jeffers: The Short Poems*, has described Jeffers' imaginary *persona* at some length.
2. See below, Chapter Six, Note 2.
3. Dr. Kiley has analyzed "Night" at length, and with interesting insights.

Chapter Four

1. See Arthur O. Lovejoy, *Essays in the History of Ideas* (Baltimore, 1948). Chapter V analyzes the different meanings of "Nature as Aesthetic Norm."
2. *Naturalism and the Human Spirit*, ed. by Y. H. Krikorian (New York, 1944), discusses the various philosophies of naturalism.
3. Edith Hamilton, *The Greek Way* (New York, 1930). Chapter 11 discusses "The Idea of Tragedy."
4. For an excellent discussion of Jeffers' use of modern non-rational psychology, see Chapter IV, "The Brain Vault," in Radcliffe Squires, *The Loyalties of Robinson Jeffers* (Ann Arbor, 1956).
5. See "'Song of Myself' as Inverted Mystical Experience," in James E. Miller, Jr. *A Critical Guide to Leaves of Grass* (Chicago, 1957).

Chapter Five

1. Quoted by permission from a letter from Mr. Jeffers to the writer, dated March 31, 1932.

Chapter Six

1. Henry W. Wells, "Grander Canyons" (see Bibliography).
2. Jeffers' theory and practice of prosody was first described by Herbert Klein, in his thesis written at Occidental College in 1930. Mr. Klein's study, in turn, was summarized and quoted by Lawrence Clark Powell in *Robinson Jeffers: the Man and his Work*, pp. 116-20. Since then comparatively little has been written on this subject.

Jeffers himself outlined his theory of prosody in 1928:

> . . . I like to avoid arbitrary form and the capricious disruption of form. My feeling is for the number of beats to the line. There is a quantitative element too in which the unstressed syllables have part. The rhythm comes from many sources—physics, biology, beat of blood, the tidal environments of life, desire for singing emphasis that prose does not have.

Jeffers' verse is never "free" in the sense that Whitman's was, and he objected to being compared to Whitman for this reason. Yet it is seldom regular in the traditional sense. It combines a feeling for accents, or stresses, with a feeling for quantity and syllables. Therefore critics of his poetry have sometimes analyzed his lines in terms of accent, sometimes in terms of quantity; I have done both with lines quoted in this book. Often the scansion of a Jeffersian line cannot be determined exactly but remains a question of individual judgment, or "ear."

Selected Bibliography

PRIMARY SOURCES

(Short publications are omitted.)

Flagons and Apples. Los Angeles: Grafton Publishing Co., 1912.

Californians. New York: Macmillan, 1916.

Tamar and Other Poems. New York: Peter G. Boyle, 1924 .

Roan Stallion, Tamar, and Other Poems. New York: Boni and Liveright, 1925. (The Modern Library reprinted this book in 1935, with a new introduction by Jeffers, and a new group of his poems never collected in other books.)

The Women at Point Sur. New York: Horace Liveright, 1927.

Cawdor and Other Poems. New York: Liveright, 1928.

Dear Judas and Other Poems. New York: Liveright, 1929.

Thurso's Landing and Other Poems. New York: Liveright, 1932.

Give Your Heart to the Hawks and Other Poems. New York: Random House, 1933.

Solstice and Other Poems. New York: Random House, 1935.

Such Counsels You Gave to Me and Other Poems. New York: Random House, 1937.

The Selected Poetry of Robinson Jeffers. New York: Random House, 1938. (Reprint of about half of the earlier poetry, including a new introduction and some new short poems.)

Be Angry at the Sun. New York: Random House, 1941.

Medea. New York: Random House, 1946.

The Double Axe and Other Poems. New York: Random House, 1948.

Hungerfield and Other Poems. New York: Random House, 1954.

SECONDARY SOURCES

A. *Books about Robinson Jeffers*

ALBERTS, S. S. *A Bibliography of the Works of Robinson Jeffers.* New York: Random House, 1933. A model bibliography, it includes a preface by Jeffers, some fragments previously unpublished, and reprints many early uncollected poems.

BENNETT, MELBA B. *Robinson Jeffers and the Sea.* San Francisco: Gelber, Lilienthal, Inc., 1936. Some personal reminiscences, and a collection of passages from Jeffers. Minor.

GILBERT, RUDOLPH. *Shine, Perishing Republic: Robinson Jeffers and the Tragic Sense in Modern Poetry.* Boston: Bruce Humphries, 1936. Miscellaneous. Includes an important letter by Jeffers.

GREENAN, EDITH. *Of Una Jeffers.* Los Angeles: Ward Ritchie Press, 1939. A vivid, personal account of Mrs. Jeffers and the early years together.

MONJIAN, MERCEDES C. *Robinson Jeffers: A Study in Inhumanism.* Pittsburgh: University of Pittsburgh Press, 1958. A thoughtful study attempting to define Jeffers' philosophy.

POWELL, LAWRENCE CLARK. *Robinson Jeffers, the Man and his Work.* Pasadena: San Pasqual Press, 1940. The best general introduction to Jeffers and his poetry. This volume supersedes two earlier books by Powell (1932,1934), although each volume contains some brief sections different from the others.

SQUIRES, RADCLIFFE. *The Loyalties of Robinson Jeffers.* Ann Arbor: University of Michigan Press, 1956. An excellent critical discussion of Jeffers' poetry and its relation to world literature.

STERLING, GEORGE. *Robinson Jeffers, the Man and the Artist.* New York: Boni and Liveright, 1926. An early appreciation by a fellow poet. Largely personal.

B. *Articles and chapters of books discussing Jeffers. (This section is highly selective.)*

ADAMIC, LOUIS. *Robinson Jeffers, a Portrait.* Seattle: University of Washington Book Store, 1929. An excellent brief, early discussion.

ANZILOTTI, ROLANDO. "Robinson Jeffers, Tragico Solitario," in *Tre Saggi Americani.* Pistoia, 1957.

CARPENTER, FREDERIC I. "Death Comes for Robinson Jeffers," *American Literature and the Dream.* New York: Philosophical Library, 1955. Jeffers' attitude toward death, and the contradictions involved.

————. "The Values of Robinson Jeffers." *American Literature,* XI (1940), 353-66.

CESTRE, CHARLES. "Robinson Jeffers." *Revue Anglo-Américaine,* IV (1927), 489-502. Excellent early criticism.

COMMAGER, HENRY STEELE. "The Cult of the Irrational," *The American Mind.* New Haven: Yale University Press, 1950. A good statement of the common-sense arguments against Jeffers.

DAVIS, HAROLD L. "Jeffers Denies Us Twice." *Poetry,* XXXI (1928), 274-79. Balanced criticism by a fellow poet.

DE CASSERES, BENJAMIN. "Robinson Jeffers, Tragic Terror." *Bookman* (November 1927), 262-66. The most enthusiastic appreciation.

FIRKINS, O. W. *"Chez Nous," The Nation,* CV (1917), 400-1. The first recognition of Jeffers by a good critic.

Selected Bibliography

GREGORY, HORACE. "Poet Without Critics: a Note on Robinson Jeffers," *New World Writing: Seventh Mentor Selection* (1955). Good, appreciative, recent criticism.

KILEY, GEORGE B. *Robinson Jeffers: The Short Poems* (Unpublished dissertation, University of Pittsburgh, 1957). Includes some excellent, original criticism.

LEHMAN, BENJAMIN H. "Robinson Jeffers." *Saturday Review of Literature*, VIII (September 5, 1931), 97. Excellent criticism of Jeffers' philosophy.

MORRIS, LLOYD S. "Robinson Jeffers: the Tragedy of a Modern Mystic," *The New Republic*, LIV (1928), 386-90. Excellent.

MOSS, SIDNEY P. "Robinson Jeffers: A Defense," *The American Book Collector*, X (September, 1959), 9-14. A good recent statement.

RODMAN, SELDEN. "Transhuman Magnificence," *Saturday Review of Literature*, XXXI (July, 1948), 13-14. Balanced criticism by a poet and anthologist.

SCHWARZ, DELMORE. "Sources of Violence," *Poetry*, LXXIII (1949), 30-38. Good negative criticism.

SHORT, R. W. "The Tower Beyond Tragedy," *Southern Review*, VII (1941), 132-44. Thoughtful, negative criticism.

VAN DOREN, MARK. "First Glance," *The Nation*, CXX (March 11, 1925), 268. Early appreciation by a poet and critic, later qualified.

WAGGONER, HYATT H. "Robinson Jeffers: Here is Reality," *The Heel of Elohim*. Norman, Okla.: University of Oklahoma Press, 1950. Good negative criticism, clearly reasoned.

————. "Science and the Poetry of Robinson Jeffers," *American Literature*, X (November, 1938), 275-88. An excellent discussion of the problem of poetry and science in the modern world.

WELLS, HENRY W. "Grander Canyons," in *The American Way of Poetry*. New York: Columbia University Press, 1943. Jeffers and the American tradition.

WILDER, AMOS. "The Nihilism of Mr. Robinson Jeffers," *Spiritual Aspects of the New Poetry*. New York: Harper and Brothers, 1940. A balanced statement by a theologian.

————. *Theology in Modern Literature*. Cambridge, Mass.: Harvard University Press, 1958. Chapter IV discusses "Dear Judas" in some detail.

WINTERS, YVOR. "Robinson Jeffers," *Poetry*, XXXV (February, 1930), 279-86. The extreme statement of negative criticism.

WOODBRIDGE, H. C. "A Bibliographical Note on Jeffers," *The American Book Collector*, X (September, 1959), 15-18. The most recent, complete bibliographical summary. Corrects and supplements earlier bibliographies since Alberts (1933).

Index

[158]